BEGIN FROM WHERE YOU ARE

ENOUGH WITH THE EXCUSES

Copyright © 2019 by Cornel Rizea
All rights reserved.
ISBN: 978-1-7321807-2-7 (print)
ISBN: 978-1-7321807-3-4 (e-book)

Cover and Interior Book Design by Inspire Books
www.inspire-books.com

Unless otherwise indicated, all Scriptures are taken from the New King James Version®. Copyright © 1982 by Thomas Nelson. Used by permission. All rights reserved.

Scripture quotations marked ESV are taken from the ESV® Bible (The Holy Bible, English Standard Version®), copyright © 2001 by Crossway, a publishing ministry of Good News Publishers. Used by permission. All rights reserved.

Scripture quotations marked NIV are taken from the Holy Bible, New International Version®, NIV®. Copyright © 1973, 1978, 1984, 2011 by Biblica, Inc.™ Used by permission of Zondervan. All rights reserved worldwide. www.zondervan.com.

Scripture quotations marked BSB are taken from the Holy Bible, Berean Study Bible, BSB. Copyright ©2016 by Bible Hub. Used by Permission. All Rights Reserved Worldwide.

Scripture quotations marked HCSB are taken from the Holman Christian Standard Bible®, Copyright © 1999, 2000, 2002, 2003, 2009 by Holman Bible Publishers. Used by permission. HCSB® is a federally registered trademark of Holman Bible Publishers.

Scripture quotations marked NASB are taken from the New American Standard Bible® (NASB). Copyright © 1960, 1962, 1963, 1968, 1971, 1972, 1973, 1975, 1977, 1995 by The Lockman Foundation. Used by permission. www.Lockman.org.

Scripture quotations marked NLT are taken from the Holy Bible, New Living Translation, copyright ©1996, 2004, 2015 by Tyndale House Foundation. Used by permission of Tyndale House Publishers, Inc., Carol Stream, Illinois 60188. All rights reserved.

BEGIN FROM WHERE YOU ARE

ENOUGH WITH THE EXCUSES

CORNEL RIZEA

I want to dedicate this book to my beautiful wife Tracey. She has been there consistently along my journey writing this, and I am truly blessed to have her in my life. Her strength, patience, love, and support have been a constant in my life, and I'm grateful beyond words. Thank you, honey. I love you to heaven and back, forever and always!

CONTENTS

Preface ix
Introduction xv
1. Personal Predicaments 1
2. Marathons and Finish Lines 9
3. Sequence Matters 15
4. Wiring Diagrams and Shot Glasses 23
5. The Greatest Attributes 31
6. The Greatest Adversaries 37
7. Precious Commodities 45
8. Oxygen Masks 53
9. The B.O.W. Improvement Process 61
10. The Most Important Thing—It's NOT about You 75

PREFACE

Today is one of the most celebrated holidays in the US. It's Thanksgiving (Thursday, November 22, 2018), and I decided to write this first paragraph on this day, at this very moment. My heart is full of gratitude for so many reasons that I wanted to begin by sharing with you some key aspects of my journey overcoming the adversity I was faced with not so long ago. My hope is that you might be able to relate to some degree, while my desire is to empower and encourage you to put away the excuses and move forward toward making improvements in your life also.

It not only seemed appropriate at this time, but the truth is that I could not procrastinate any longer. I wanted to get going right now by practicing what I'm about to preach, so to speak. I wanted to put away all my excuses and hopefully lead by example. I wanted to begin this new project precisely from where I happen to be in my life on this very day.

It goes without saying that being thankful is not limited to the Thanksgiving holiday each year. Living in a free society where one is able to pursue his or her own happiness can absolutely be reason for daily appreciation. I'm sure we're all aware of the powerful phrase found in the US Declaration of Independence, where it states that every American has the right to "Life, Liberty and the pursuit of Happiness." It is one of the main reasons I feel so incredibly fortunate. Certainly, this should be a reason to put a smile on anyone's face. The expression has been said many times and is perhaps worth repeating again: *Is this a great country or what?*

I referred to this undertaking—my second book—as a new project. Actually, when I think about it, I can honestly describe it as *a labor of love.* I enjoy sharing with others what has helped me overcome adversity in the recent past, while continuing to do so to this very day. The goal is to describe this in a respectful manner and not in any sort of boastful way. I aim to do it in a way that is real, relatable, relevant, and helpful, yet does not sugarcoat the subject. There is perhaps no greater reward than knowing that, somehow, you had a positive effect on someone else's life.

Earlier this year, I had just finished publishing my first book, *"CITIZEN of HEAVEN—No Waiting Period Required."* Although it had only been made available to the public for a relatively short time, I had received lots of heartwarming comments from most everyone I knew who read it, as well as from total strangers. Somewhat surprised at first, I was also asked quite a few times when the next book would be coming out. My answer, at least for the first few months, was very consistent. No more books. I was done writing.

It took me so long to get all that down on paper, I reasoned to myself. It was a difficult subject, and I wasn't even sure how the message would be received. I had just been through an emotional rollercoaster ride. The research seemed never-ending. It took a lot more energy than I originally thought it would. On and on and on, I explained my position. As it turned out, those were all excuses, and I knew it.

I had begun that original journey taking on that first project because I felt the subject was not only personal, but the main message was, and still is, of enormous importance for all of us mere mortals. I wanted my kids and anyone else who read it to have no doubt about where I personally stood on the subject of God, creation, and heaven. I wanted to share what I believe is still the main problem in the world today, as well as the greatest news that could possibly exist.

Just as importantly, I also wanted others to learn about the immeasurable importance of the final eternal destination of every human being's soul. It had taken me just under seven years to complete that little book. During the research and the process of putting my thoughts together along the way, I had learned a lot about the subject and about myself, as well as about the vast nature of things in general. As much as I enjoyed the ride of expressing myself in writing, I just couldn't see myself considering doing that again, certainly not anytime soon.

Fast-forward to where I am today, just a few short months later. I must admit that after it was all said and done, writing turned out to be an extremely gratifying experience. It was also very humbling, to say the least. I knew down deep that I was mainly doing it for the benefit of anyone who cared enough to open their eyes and contemplate the magnitude of the subject matter. It was a sort of calling, which I felt compelled to pursue so that others might benefit. After all, what could be better than sharing a *win-win* situation?

"So, when is the next one coming out?" my editor asked. "I'm done," was my immediate reply. Isn't it funny how these brief interactions and subliminal suggestions can sometimes take on a life of their own?

During the past few months, I found myself trying to dismiss the thoughts that I noticed had begun swirling around in my mind. Once again, I was being pulled toward another idea that I thought could also help others. In my recent experiences, I had noticed a continuous pattern of improvement from a dire situation I was in a few years ago. I then began thinking about sharing that pattern and some of these experiences with others to help them progress from their own place in life. I wanted to share a bit more of my story and describe some of my own journey from a place that seemed pretty hopeless at the time.

What is it that prevents some people from improving their situation? I would ask myself at times. It seemed to me that some people were stuck in a deep rut. Not always, but at times perhaps, the situation they found themselves in was through no fault of their own. Or perhaps there were other reasons why they were stuck that they were totally responsible for. Regardless of how they got into the rut, perhaps they could do something about it but didn't know where to begin.

Those were my initial thoughts. I knew painfully well the situation I had found myself in just a few years ago, and I also knew the difficulties and challenges I faced along the way. It took some time for me to arrive at a much more pleasant place. So, it started. I was once again compelled to share my thoughts, ideas, and parts of my journey, as well as some conclusions on the pages of this, my second book. Slowly but surely, I arrived at the point where I could no longer resist the heartfelt desire to share what I know has helped me along the way.

Here we go again, I thought to myself. I was just going about my daily routines, minding my own business, when suddenly I caught myself jotting things down on loose pieces of paper. Some of these other ideas and thoughts were beginning to take shape with hints of increasing clarity as time marched forward. Right about that time, I recalled the recent words from some people who were asking about the possibility of a next book.

I had heard that most authors usually follow through with at least one other book. Somewhere along the way, I was advised that when—not if—thoughts of another book came along, I should not dismiss them. I continue to remain humbled by the very kind words my editor shared with me. Among other comments, I was simply encouraged to be open to the idea of writing again, and that I would know when the time was right. This was definitely that time.

The common denominator as far as motivation for me to write again was the same this time. My sincere desire was then, as it is today, to write about something that will help someone. I decided to write again because I wanted you, the reader, to benefit from it. I wanted to reveal to you the principles which I found to be powerful, comforting, and true when I felt lost, confused, deceived, deserted, trapped, alone, and in major debt. I wanted to empower you by sharing my experiences with you so that you might benefit as well. I wanted to remind you that every single day is a precious gift that you should not waste, and it's never too late to improve your situation, no matter how dire it may seem to you.

I wanted to encourage you to take the steps needed to improve your circumstances, because others in your circle of influence can also benefit as you, in turn, pay it forward. I wanted to share with you the process that I found to be extremely helpful during a time in my life when I thought the world was coming to an end. I wanted to challenge you to put away all the excuses and show that you, too, can **begin from where you are.**

Cornel Rizea

INTRODUCTION

Everyone has a story. We each have a personal path that led us to the place where we happen to be. There is no misunderstanding on my part that each of our paths had twists and turns and hills and valleys and rocky roads and some parts that were perhaps a bit smoother. At this very moment, I happen to be writing these words, and you happen to be reading them. Our paths seem to be intersecting, if only for a brief period.

All our individual stories are unique, and every story matters to each of us in a very personal way. We all arrived at the point where we happen to be in our lives by zigzagging our way here. Regardless of how we got here, it's probably safe to say that nobody has brought us to our current place in life by brute force. In other words, we each must conclude that we ourselves had something to do with our current destination.

Perhaps we happen to have been at a location where an incident happened that changed everything. Maybe we were scammed into doing this or that. Maybe we were conned out of something. Maybe we listened to this person or that person for some reason, and it turned out to be a complete lie. Maybe we took advantage of a situation that sounded too good to be true, then not surprisingly, it turned out to be exactly that. Maybe we lived here or there because of the circumstances. Maybe we went to this or that school or no school at all, for whatever reason. Maybe we didn't get the job we thought was perfect, or maybe we missed the investment that was going to make all the pain go away.

Some of us can come up with unique scenarios in which certain events that negatively affected our lives took place without our knowledge or even our consent. That could certainly be the case when we were younger. Be that as it may, it's safe to say that we somehow found ourselves in certain situations where we had to make an evaluation of what was going on and then decide our next move. We were put in a situation and had no choice but to dig ourselves out of it. One can say that we were each confronted with different challenges in life. We each made choices, at least for the most part, that we thought would benefit us somehow in the long run.

There is absolutely nobody else who has walked in your shoes, nor has anyone else walked in mine. It's impossible for anyone else to understand exactly what you've experienced along the way. It's also virtually impossible for anyone to completely see the reasons you may be feeling either stuck or dissatisfied. It's also fair to say that we can all do our best to relate, or at least try to imagine to some extent, as we empathize when we hear of someone else's predicament. We're all human, and we should never forget that. We can express compassion, and we can mourn for a period, then we can hold our head up again, smile, and work for a better tomorrow.

Having said all that, now what? As far as what we do next, does it really matter how we got here in the first place? Sure, it matters to the extent that you know what happened, but dwelling on it won't get you out of it. If you spilled some milk on the floor, then mopping it up as soon as possible would not only prevent a slippery hazard right away, but it would also help you move forward as well as help you forget about the lost milk. You certainly must have heard the expression, "It's how you react that's important." Life is not always fair, but nobody ever promised it would be. No matter what situation you happen to find yourself in today, I'm a believer that things can get better not only for you but for others all around you within your circle of influence.

If we really want to improve our individual circumstances, we should admit where we are, learn from one another, help one another, encourage one another, and take action to help ourselves and make things better. I'd like to add emphasis to the key phrase here: *if we really want to improve*. On second thought, I'd like to replace that phrase with *if we really understood how to improve*. Helping you understand the *how* part was front and center on my mind when I decided to write this book.

Yes, I happen to be in the camp that believes that each of us would have a much better chance to improve our own situation if we took the time to understand *how*. What does it take to get out of the mess we're in? Perhaps we could improve even more if we learned from the past and took the time to prevent the same thing from happening in the future. What I'm trying to say in all this is that *gaining understanding is a fundamental prerequisite to making improvements*.

In biblical times, there were none like King Solomon. It's worth noting that he asked God to bless him with a *wise and understanding heart*. If you were to decide to read the book of Proverbs, written by King Solomon himself, I have no doubt you'd find that God certainly answered his prayer.

Irrespective of where you happen to be today, I'm convinced that we all need to seek to gain a better understanding of any situation we find ourselves in, especially when it comes to making continual improvements in our lives. Once that understanding is established, then repeating that process and applying it to other circumstances becomes much easier over time. The level of any noticeable improvement in any area of your life will be in direct proportion to the level of understanding gained on that subject. Bear with me for just a moment as I ask that you allow that statement to sink in by repeating it:

> ***The level of improvement in any area of your life will be in direct proportion to the level of understanding gained on that subject.***

If, for whatever reason, you feel stuck in an unpleasant situation while spinning your wheels in one spot with little to no progress, my goal is to show you a way to improve so that you can get unstuck and move ahead toward a better place. I want to explain and spell out a very simple, yet very helpful, process that I found to be straightforward and applicable to many situations.

What I'm hoping for is that it will make sense to you so that you can use it too. I want to also make it easy to understand, and I want it to somehow resonate with your way of thinking so that it will cause you to take action right away. The best part is that this improvement process is repeatable. I really do believe that every situation can be improved, so I decided to do my part and share with you what I did. I wanted to pass on to you what worked for me.

The time feels right. I will do my very best to present to you my thoughts and ideas from my perspective on what it takes to improve a situation in practically any area of your life. Making things better can be rewarding in many ways, so let's do our best to put away all the excuses that have held us back for so long. For some of us, the excuses have become nothing but crutches for us to lean on while remaining stuck.

The answers to the questions below may seem obvious, but I'd like to ask them anyway. If you read through the rest of the chapters, you will find that I have a reason for spelling out these questions in the beginning.

- Do you want to be healthier?
- Do you want to have more joy in your life?
- Do you want to live with less stress?
- Do you want more meaningful relationships?
- Do you want to earn more money?
- Do you want to be a business owner?
- Do you want to be financially independent?
- Do you want to be debt-free?
- Do you want to have more free time?

- Do you want to own your dream house?
- Do you want to live in a better neighborhood?
- Do you want to go on more vacations?
- Do you want to retire more comfortably?
- Do you want more peace of mind?
- Do you want to be more charitable?
- Do you want to add more value to other people's lives?
- Do you want to be a better son, daughter, spouse, sibling, parent, friend, employee, employer, coworker, or teammate?
- Do you want to end up in heaven after you take your last breath on earth?

There is nothing out of the ordinary about these questions, as we are all trying our very best to improve our standard of living and the quality of our daily lives. The desired outcome I'm hoping for is that you will be able to relate in some way and apply the themes of the following chapters to make things better for you and your loved ones. I will have accomplished my goal if any of what I have written causes you to advance toward a more comfortable and happier place in your life.

Know for sure that you're not alone in thinking that it's difficult dealing with the challenges we each face constantly in our daily lives. Also know for sure that *difficult* does not mean *impossible*; that distinction should give you courage and hope. If it were easy, we would likely agree that we would all have resolved most of our problems by now.

The situation for some is worse than for others, but things can certainly get better for anyone, no matter what their starting point is. Improvement takes time, but it's never too late to begin. The main theme is *to begin*. Even though some cases may be more challenging than others, the reward of accomplishing gradual yet noticeable improvements will be well worth the effort once you decide to take the necessary first steps.

With that out of the way, why don't more people just go right ahead and take the steps needed to make things better for themselves? It appears that most can certainly make progress, but it doesn't seem to be working. It sometimes seems that they find it easier to remain complacent in that rut while only generating complaints that land on deaf ears. Perhaps they're not sure of where to start, or perhaps there is an unrealistic expectation of immediate gratification. In a lot of cases, it's certainly not from a lack of spending energy trying.

I don't for a moment want to even pretend to understand the dire predicaments some people are faced with every day. One only has to turn on the news to hear tragic stories of real problems people all over the globe are dealing with on an ongoing basis. With that in mind, I would like to humbly offer a suggestion that maybe, just maybe, if you're reading the words in this book, you will be able to find some helpful and comforting ideas that will lead to some relief in your life.

Just to give you a brief introduction to this improvement process, which I still use, I have categorized it in three distinct phases. It is my experience that the second and third phases build on the previous one(s) to form a solid foundation for perpetual improvement. I have also found that if I exclude any of the three phases of the improvement process, then the results will be limited at best. I refer to this improvement process using the acronym B.O.W.

B = Believe
O = Observe
W = Will

I will go into much more detail on each of these three phases in a later chapter, but for now, I want to introduce you to my starting point. I want to help you see a few of the challenges I found myself in at one point in my life, not so long ago. I want to share with you what worked and how it worked and why it worked for me. I want to explain how I arrived at the B.O.W. improvement process. Most importantly, even though our starting points are different, I am hopeful that you will be able to relate in some way. At the end of the day, I'm confident that the B.O.W. improvement process can very likely help you too.

So, what do you say? Would you like to learn what worked for me, even though my personal predicament is very likely different from yours? Let's go through this together. Let's put away all the excuses and allow ourselves to gain understanding of why we should implement the B.O.W. improvement process. I'm hopeful that if you decide to invest the time it takes to read and grasp the ideas in the next several chapters, you will be motivated to take positive steps toward a better place for yourself.

1
PERSONAL PREDICAMENTS

There are many memorable moments in life, but perhaps few such occurrences can be described as major or defining moments. For me, one of the most—or perhaps *the* most—defining moments took place during an early evening in October 1999. I came home from work, and the tension in the air seemed thick—yet another day. I didn't like that feeling at all, but I didn't really know what to do about it. I didn't quite understand how it got to that point. It seemed that no matter what words I used to begin a conversation with my wife, they seemed to be met with brief, empty remarks.

I took our four young kids to McDonald's that evening, as my wife didn't want to join us. When we got back home, I found the letter my wife had written to me. The Cole's Notes, or CliffsNotes, version of her letter was that it was over between us. Our youngest was barely out of diapers by this point and my wife, seemingly straight out of the blue, claimed that it was now *her* time. To say that there was a tsunami of emotions flooding every cell of my entire being would be a tremendous understatement. The events about to unfold from that point forward were the furthest things from my mind. I thought the world was unraveling at the seams. Nothing made sense. *This could have never happened to me and my family*, were my only thoughts at the time. I was obviously wrong.

To go through a play-by-play of the very odd, strange, and deceptive events during the following year would be completely pointless for the purpose of this book. I have since put them all in the rearview mirror as a distant memory. They're all like water that flowed under the proverbial bridge a long time ago. At this point, those events will neither add anything of value to my message here, nor are they worth repeating. Needless to say, I was most concerned at the time for our kids, and the impact this would have on their young, impressionable minds.

I will only say that despite all the schemes used throughout the divorce process, I tried my best to always keep a certain thought front and center in my mind, no matter what. I recall reminding myself on many occasions that somehow, it will be ok. I certainly didn't know how, but I simply maintained that *this too shall pass.*

So, this was the place from which I began. This was my starting line. This was my personal predicament and my defining moment. I had just turned forty and suddenly found myself alone with visitation rights for my kids while under the indescribable weight of a gigantic mountain of debt. The constant feelings I was trying to hide ranged from total confusion to utter hopelessness. I recall feeling worse for our four young kids who were all innocently watching all this unfolding.

I have to say that during that time of personal distress, my immediate family was extremely supportive to the very best of their ability, and I will forever be grateful. I read a couple of helpful books that my older sister gave me, I reflected a lot, I immersed myself in my work, I drove about four hours to attend a relationship seminar, I cried, I laughed, I pondered, and I prayed. I also took a flight to Florida to talk with my older brother who lived there with his family. I needed to try and shake the cobwebs I felt trapped in. My brain seemed to be in a fog; everything was happening in slow motion for some reason. I'm sure I was in denial of the reality of the situation I had just found myself in.

For the few days that I was in Florida, I drove to the East Coast early each morning to watch the sunrise. I'd spend hours there just staring out to the ocean, listening to the waves crashing down on the beach. Each evening, I drove to the West Coast and watched the sunset, wondering if the world was coming to an end. Day after day, the sun kept coming up, so, for the time being anyway, I slowly dismissed the end-of-the-world scenario. I was trying to make some sense of it all. I was looking for some sort of sign as to what to do next.

Then one day, it happened. While I was contemplating moving to Florida, perhaps trying to escape my reality, I heard my brother ask me the question, "What about the kids?" That was it. The fog I had been in began to thin out. I just knew in that very moment what I needed to do next. It's not like I had forgotten about my kids, but somehow that question broke the chains that seemed to have kept my mind hostage up to that point.

I ended up flying back and, shortly thereafter, took my kids out for ice cream while doing my best to assure them that things would be OK. I wanted to make sure they all knew that I wasn't going anywhere. For some unexplainable reason, I began to believe that it would all work out somehow. Admittedly, I had no idea how that better state would come about. What I do recall is that I began keeping a vision in my mind where things would not only settle down, they would improve. I wasn't afraid of the unknown anymore. I started asking, "What if?" a lot. I began believing in the possibility of a better tomorrow, and that gave me hope and energy to look further into what I could do about it.

From that point forward, it didn't seem to matter any longer that I didn't really understand or agree with all the events that had led to the current situation I found myself in. The fact that nothing made any sense was completely irrelevant now. I recall thinking at the time that all that mattered was for me to focus any free time I had on taking baby steps toward that better place that I envisioned in my mind. No more complaining. No more blaming. No more negative thoughts. No more feeling sorry for myself. No more what-ifs. No more indecisiveness. *No more excuses.*

I recall wondering where the best place would be for me to begin the journey toward recovery. The choices were so many. Looking back now, I think I was simply looking for something, anything, that could immediately alleviate my grief. I was looking for a path to ease the pressures of the seemingly insurmountable huge mountain of debt I was suddenly faced with.

There is no question that your personal predicament is different from mine. Sure, some aspects may be similar, but they are certainly not the same. Each person's situation involves different people with different circumstances. These situations may happen to someone earlier in life or perhaps later, toward their golden years. They may have something to do with health, work, family members, strangers, businesses, accidents, money, fraud, theft, living arrangements, or any other life-altering event you can think of.

I've heard it said that we all have some scars, even though they are not all visible. Some people have larger scars than other people. Although the scars can be physical or emotional or both, they are reminders that we were once wounded but we were not overcome. I have always thought that this distinction mattered. *That which doesn't kill you makes you stronger* is a popular phrase.

The scars were all caused by the personal predicaments we each found ourselves in at one time or another. We can reflect, we can talk about the scars, we can learn from what happened, and we can take steps to move forward toward a better place. This, of course, assumes that you have allowed for the wound to heal, even though the scar may still be there. Notice I mentioned that *you* needed to allow for the wound to heal.

On the other hand, if the wound is still open, the situation should be addressed immediately so infections don't set in and debilitate you. The exterior bleeding may have been dealt with, but there may still be internal bleeding going on, both literally and figuratively. I mean, how long should it take for a wound to heal? I suppose one could rightfully say that it depends on the wound.

A better question might be, how long will you allow yourself to limit your potential because you were once wounded? How many ways would you like to explain your position and remain in pain? Will anything you come up with really matter anytime soon? How much longer will you continue to wander in the past? What is the average length of time a pity party lasts anyway? Is there a timer that sounds off somewhere giving you a clue that *it's time* and the wound is now scheduled to be healed?

The last thing I want to do is minimize what you have gone through, so please don't take it that way. I readily admit that I have no right to do that, as I have not walked in your shoes. What I am honestly trying to do in writing this book is to spell out that maybe, just maybe, you can try a different path forward. To that end, I am going to share with you in the following chapters the insights that led me to the B.O.W. process toward recovery that I found to be so helpful, before I ask you to consider implementing it in your own life.

Again, it's been said many times that it's not the things that happen to you, but how you react to those things that are important. I promised a friend of mine that I would quote him when he told me his secret to moving ahead was to simply *let it go*. On the surface, that sounds pretty good, right? Let's just all let go of the pain. The question, obviously, is *how*. How do you let go of something that affected your life in such a personal way and move toward a happier place? Perhaps it's easier said than done, but for now, let's just agree to consider that it is possible. This may also be a good place for all of us to be reminded that doing the same thing while expecting different results is, well, insanity.

People from all walks of life are hurting in many unique ways. We all need to begin moving forward from where we happen to be, so letting go of some unproductive baggage sounds like a pretty good suggestion to lighten our load. This doesn't mean that the incident responsible for the scar was OK, nor does it mean that it didn't hurt. Most importantly, if it didn't kill us, it also means that we are not helpless and totally incapable of altering the course of events going forward. It doesn't have to have the last word on the rest of our lives.

So, here we are. We each have our personal stories as well as our personal predicaments that led us to the place where we happen to find ourselves at this very moment. So, what now? Where do we begin to get some relief? What do we do first? I'm going to humbly suggest that we start by looking in the mirror and taking ownership of the place we're in right now, regardless of how we got here. I would also challenge you to dig in your heels and declare that enough is enough. Dare to believe that improvement can be achieved in spite of the scars. Dare to generate a vision of a happier place. Do your very best to maintain laser focus on that vision, regardless of the difficulties that lie ahead. Let's all embark on the recovery journey together. Let's all move forward and make things better.

Reflection Questions for Chapter 1:

1. What is or was the most challenging defining moment in your life that caused you grief?

   _____
   _____
   _____
   _____
   _____
   _____
   _____
   _____
   _____
   _____
   _____

2. What were the thoughts and fears going through your mind during that time?

   _____
   _____
   _____
   _____
   _____
   _____
   _____
   _____
   _____
   _____
   _____
   _____

2
MARATHONS AND FINISH LINES

It was late fall of 2011 when a couple of people I was working with started a conversation about marathons. The young lady in our workgroup had already completed a few marathons and was preparing for yet another one. She described in some detail not just the physical and mental preparation but also the routine sacrifices needed to get to the starting line. The other guy in our group was describing what he had just experienced, having completed a local half marathon earlier that same year. I joined the conversation, and for some unexplainable reason, the marathon seed took root and almost immediately began to sprout some whispers of, *I think I can do this*.

The thought of running a marathon was never on my radar, and certainly not on any sort of bucket list up until that point. Sure, I ran some track events in grade school and high school, but I wasn't a long-distance runner by any stretch of the imagination. I recall having watched some highlights of the ironman competitions in Hawaii and other parts of the world. The demands on a person's mind and body to complete a full ironman triathlon is certainly impressive and can only be accurately described by those who have been there. Some of the stories of the participants were nothing short of inspiring and spiritually uplifting.

The full ironman triathlon consists of a 2.4-mile swim, followed by a 112-mile bicycle ride, then finally a 26.2-mile run, raced in that order and without a break. To put the difficulty of this event in perspective, it is estimated that out of about 7.3 billion people living on earth, only about 0.007 percent have completed a full ironman triathlon. That happens to be some very rare company.

As for completing *only* the full 26.2-mile run, it is estimated that about 0.5 percent of the US population have run this marathon race. There was something about the challenge of completing such an event that was captivating to me. As I announced that I would begin training for a full marathon, people learned that I had never completed a half marathon before, nor even a 10k race of any sort. My honest reply to anyone who asked me about my decision was that I wanted to experience the full effect of a full marathon. My goal was simply to survive and live to tell about it. Little did I know at the time that I'd be writing about what I learned in the process.

Along with all the positive thoughts of *I think I can do this*, I must admit that I also had some reservations. I read about what it took to complete a full marathon. I got more educated about physical conditioning, as well as the importance of having your mind engaged in the right way. I began some basic training, but it was not quite as prescribed in the book. According to the average training required, I should have started a lot sooner in order to participate in the marathon, which was scheduled for early spring of 2012.

I talked with other runners and got their insights from their experiences. Shortly into the physical training routine, I wondered many times what exactly I had signed up for. Training took a lot of my spare time after work and on weekends. I also wondered why I wanted to do this in the first place and even second-guessed myself on a few occasions when quitting altogether crossed my mind. I would contemplate the reason (excuse) I would be prepared to tell everyone who knew I had signed up for the marathon, just in case I decided to back out of my public commitment. In retrospect, I'm glad that even though these thoughts were present, I didn't speak these words of doubt during that time to anyone.

I resolved my self-doubts by the fact that I only had control of one day at a time. Every day, I was faced with a choice of what to do with any of the spare time I had at my disposal. Some days I squeezed in a twenty-minute training session, other days it was a two-hour session. Many times, I was even jogging in the basement of our house from one end to the other, just to continue to take advantage of my available time, no matter where I was. The training during the winter months of 2011 were spent mostly indoors. Even though each session brought about its own flavor of difficulty, I noticed that my confidence level to complete the race was increasing. My original thought and belief that *I think I can do this* grew stronger every day, and it morphed into conviction.

By late February into early March 2012, my thoughts were *I believe I can complete this marathon* and *I know I can do this because I'm prepared*. I knew that I wouldn't break any records that day, but survival was a likely outcome. I also knew that I had done my very best, given all my circumstances and time constraints. Those were now the thoughts swirling around my mind as the anticipated April 2012 race day approached.

Before the race began, I recall looking up at the starting line, just breathing calmly, knowing all the time, energy, and preparation that had gone in prior to that day. I was glad to be there among the participants, for sure. I suddenly found myself in the middle of hundreds of other runners jogging forward, some at a slower pace, and some faster than me. As I ran across the starting line, I thought about how brief, yet very relevant, that moment in time was, when the timer recorded my bib crossing the starting line. It was just the beginning. The real challenge of the 26.2-mile run was ahead.

The race course consisted of various sections, which, as I'm sure you can imagine, were straight, curved, flat, angled, and hilly. The challenges of the terrain and surface conditions on the course were the same for everyone. All participants had to face these difficulties according to their individual training and preparation. The weather throughout the day also varied. It started out on the chilly side in the morning, then it turned sunny and a bit muggy, followed by some light drizzle and wind toward the end of the race. Everyone had to constantly adjust and stay alert to the changing conditions as the race progressed.

I noticed that there was a lot of encouragement along the way as well. We passed through neighborhoods where people were lined up cheering and supporting the runners. Water stations were set up every two miles to give the runners a chance to grab some nourishment and water to go. I frequently walked through these watering stations while monitoring and evaluating my physical ability to proceed to the next station.

I also observed that some runners kept jogging right through the water stations, while others were stooped over a table or crouched down trying to recover and catch their breath. I heard many times that day from the spectators, from the staffers, and also from among us runners, "You can do this" and "One more station" and "You've only got a bit more to go" and "Don't give up." Everyone in the race settled into their individual pace. It didn't take long for me to realize that most of the runners had goals similar to mine. We all wanted to complete the race to the very best of our ability, and, yes, also survive to tell about it.

Crossing the finish line was an exhilarating experience. It was physically, mentally, and emotionally exhausting to get there, but it was extremely gratifying at the same time. There was a sense of relief and accomplishment when the medal for completion was awarded. The sore muscles seemed to begin healing immediately. I heard someone mention, "You're a marathoner now." It was certainly worth the effort. Shortly after I got home that day, I wobbled into the house and promptly announced my retirement from any future marathons.

In the previous chapter, I gave you a brief description of the predicament that essentially turned my life upside down. This was my personal starting line from which I entered the road toward making things better. This was the place from which my recovery journey began. No doubt you're starting from a different line. Our situations perhaps may be similar, but it's safe to say that they're also different.

In this chapter, I shared a bit about my 26.2-mile-race experience. The point was not for you go out and run a marathon yourself, although you may end up doing just that if you want to. The point was for me to share the lessons I learned along the way: lessons of acceptance, humility, belief, research, hard work, conviction, perseverance, encouragement, and hope.

I've heard it said that life itself resembles a marathon, as opposed to a sprint. We need to pause and realize that we're in this long-distance run for a while, so we need some training and conditioning for endurance and longevity. It would be helpful for us to have some understanding of what it takes to safely navigate through the marathon of life with a bit more ease. Things happen sometimes in our lives without our permission or knowledge, and perhaps without our involvement. It's what we do from that point forward that really matters. In that sense, every day is a brand-new starting line. It's a fresh beginning and a new opportunity to learn and train.

Although the starting lines for the marathon of each of our lives may be in different locations, life still moves forward for all of us around the globe. We all wind our way through the ups and downs of life to the very best of our abilities. To use the same analogy, the ease with which we can move forward in the marathon of life depends on our training and preparation, *prior to having arrived at the starting line.*

As for the finish line for the marathon of life on earth, unlike the 26.2-mile run, it's the day we take our last breath, although I assume that some would likely debate that too. Suffice it to say that for the purpose of this chapter, the main message is straightforward. We should each take advantage of opportunities in our spare time and continually train and better condition ourselves by gaining understanding of the things we're dealing with at our individual starting lines. Preparation is undoubtedly essential for a less stressful time during this marathon called life.

Reflection Questions for Chapter 2:

1. What event comes to mind for which you invested a lot of time to be better prepared?

   _____
   _____
   _____
   _____
   _____
   _____
   _____
   _____
   _____
   _____
   _____
   _____

2. What sacrifices did you make along the way?

   _____
   _____
   _____
   _____
   _____
   _____
   _____
   _____
   _____
   _____
   _____
   _____

3
SEQUENCE MATTERS

There is something that absolutely matters if you want to make progress, regardless of where your starting line is. One could argue that it's even critical to your long-term well-being. I'm talking about the order—the sequence—in which you tend to tackle problems on a regular basis. Yes, this sounds pretty basic, yet it is widely overlooked. Taking the time to organize your thoughts and follow-up actions regarding your situation will have a huge impact on how long you will either continue to suffer due to your predicament, or how quickly you can begin solving your problems and moving forward.

The sequence in which you begin to resolve life's challenges matters, perhaps more than you realize, to you personally as well as those in your circle of influence. When there are many things going on in your life, they all seem to be trying to grab your attention, and it can get overwhelming. You could give them all equal importance, but that gets really confusing, really fast. What should you focus on first? Which of these items needs your immediate attention and which can be put on the back burner? How do you prioritize? In this case, ignorance is anything but bliss.

We can all relate to the fact that life is constantly throwing some sort of curveball our way. I've also heard some people make comments that more curveballs seem to be headed their way than toward others. What is going on around here? Oh no, not again, not another one! Life is just not fair, they might add. They might even jokingly assert that if they didn't know any better, they'd say they actually attract curveballs. That last statement could be true, but I doubt it.

A lot of people are frustrated that they can't seem to catch a break. Undoubtedly every situation can be dissected for what's really going on, but here's what I've found that most people don't really want to hear. I found that fewer and fewer people are prepared to deal with the curveballs. What's probably worse, they don't even want to hear how ill prepared they really are. Fewer people are ready for it when the ball is crossing the plate. When people can't handle the curveballs effectively, they continue to get bombarded from all angles.

Have you ever seen, or do you know of, someone who looked extremely busy working away at something only to find out later that it was a complete waste of time? Maybe after the fact it was discovered that the work didn't need to be done at all. Maybe the person wasn't qualified in the first place, and the work completed didn't pass the necessary quality checks. Maybe shortcuts were taken, and the work that the person just completed had to be undone so it could be redone correctly. Has it even happened to you perhaps? I'm alluding to the importance of thinking and doing things in the proper sequence.

Someone spread a truckload of mulch in a large landscaping project only to find out that the weed-prevention fabric should have been laid down before the mulch was applied.

Someone cemented all the fence posts in shallow holes in the ground only to find that the first winter frost caused the posts to be pushed up, collapsing the fence.

Someone connected an entire water piping system only to find out that water leaked at all the fittings and joints because no gaskets were used.

Someone built a house only to find that the foundation walls developed cracks due to improper preparation of the subsurface the footings were mounted on.

Someone got stopped for making an illegal left turn only to find out that the car insurance was expired.

Someone pulled over on a rural road because of a flat tire, only to find out that the nearest town was 250 miles away and the spare tire was also flat.

Someone gambled away his $500 paycheck at a nearby casino only to find a reminder text from his wife, who was waiting for him to bring home groceries.

Someone wanted to save a few bucks for the company by purchasing *similar* fasteners for their product only to find out that all products failed across the nation due to the cheaper inferior fasteners.

Someone put the proverbial cart before the horse. I think you get the idea by now.

Of course, nobody is perfect, and mistakes can and do happen. Some mistakes result in no significant damage, while others end in catastrophic disaster. The main takeaway is for us to learn from the past, then take the necessary steps to make the correct adjustments and move forward toward a better future. On the other hand, repeating similar mistakes is a whole different story. Continuing down this path can certainly delay progress, increase the cost of repairs, and possibly paralyze you from taking any action at all.

Yes, we're all human, and we can all relate to the humbling impact of our mistakes. We can certainly make a mess of a situation from time to time in spite of our best intentions. I'll be the first to admit that I've eaten my share of humble pie on a few memorable occasions, just like everyone else. In those situations, I've done my best to reverse course as soon as I could, so at least the pie was still fresh.

I have witnessed individuals from all walks of life trying to accomplish various things using some very strange approaches. For whatever reason, they seemed to go about it in such a way that the resulting damage was sometimes quite excessive. Those losses would be hard to swallow, but nonetheless that situation became the person's *new and improved* starting point. I have also heard of others working away at resolving something that wasn't even the problem to begin with. They didn't even bother to investigate the cause of the problem.

We all learn new skills in a series of steps, and these steps need to be presented in the right sequence. An apprentice becomes a licensed carpenter after having completed some classroom work, as well as some hands-on practical experience under a proficient supervisor. This all takes time. You could try to save some money and hire someone with zero carpentry background to build a six-foot-tall wood fence along the perimeter of your backyard, but you'd be asking for a disaster. In other words, such a request would make no sense because of the obvious consequences.

Sure, the skills needed to build a fence can be obtained, but like anything else worthwhile, it takes some time. Most importantly, the person must be willing to learn the skills and then perform the tasks needed in the right sequence in order to complete the fence.

A similar process of executing sequential steps applies to making any sort of improvement in our daily lives. We gain expertise at something through mastering a series of sequential, gradual steps. It may seem difficult or feel strange at first, but each conquered step helps us gain confidence as we begin to see improvements. This, in turn, encourages us to keep moving forward with greater ease.

Learning is not the same as teaching. If a person is qualified to teach a subject, this does not mean the lesson will be automatically learned. Even if the teacher is enthusiastic in presenting the lesson or has all kinds of pertinent examples to demonstrate the validity of the lesson, we would all agree that the person being presented with the lesson—the one who is supposed to be learning—must be willing to receive its content. In simple terms, the person must be willing to learn. I've heard it said many times that *there is no teaching, only learning.* How true that is.

It's the learning that is paramount. If you want to learn how to improve something in your life, there is absolutely no shortage of advice. When it comes to the sequence of tasks on the path to improvement, learning is at the top. On the other hand, if you're not willing to learn something that may be helpful to your personal predicament, then, well, have a nice day! I honestly wish you all the best.

If you're not willing to learn about a subject, then maybe it's not something you're interested in. Perhaps the problem isn't big enough for you to learn how to deal with it right away. I mean, why learn something today if you can put it off till tomorrow? Maybe the problem will go away by then, so why rush into this? Perhaps you may think you already know all about that particular subject, so there is nothing new for you to learn. However, if similar problems persist in your life, my guess is that you may be distracted by a host of other items that have piled up over time because they were not dealt with properly early enough.

It's worth repeating once again that, generally, it's not the things that happen in your life, it's how you react to them that counts. I have personally experienced various negative events in my life, as I'm sure you have also. Even though the events in our lives are different, reacting to them in the right way and in the right sequence matters more than we realize. Take the time to learn as much as you can about the situation first. Everything else will fall in line.

- Learning the specifics of the situation leads to knowledge.
- Knowledge leads to wisdom.
- Wisdom allows for the correct application of the knowledge gained.
- Correct application leads to effective behaviors.
- Repetition of effective behaviors leads to good habits.

- Good habits lead to desired outcomes or improvements.
- Improvements lead to confidence in the process.

As you continue to learn more about each of the predicaments you face, you will build a solid foundation on which you can stand firm with less stress. Sooner than you may think, you will be much better prepared to handle the curveballs life throws your way.

I want to end this chapter with the story of a professor of Psychology 101 addressing new students on their very first day of class. The professor walked to the front of the classroom without saying a word. He started by taking a large glass jar from underneath his desk and placing it on the desk for everyone to see. Just as every student settled in, watching the front of the classroom, the professor took some large rocks he had staged there and proceeded to insert all the rocks one by one into the jar, to the very top. He then looked up and asked the class, "Is the jar full?" The students, looking intently at what was going on, spoke up, saying, "Yes, the jar is full."

Without answering the class, the professor looked under his desk and brought up a bag full of pebbles. He then slowly poured the bag of pebbles into the jar. As he shook the jar a bit, all the smaller pebbles found their way into the voids between the rocks, up to the very top of the jar. The professor once again asked, "Is the jar full?" The students looked at each other, and once again agreed, "Yes, the jar is full."

Once again, the professor, without addressing the class, reached underneath his desk and pulled up a bag of sand. As he poured the bag of sand into the jar, all the remaining voids between the pebbles and the rocks filled up with the much smaller grains of sand. The professor again looked up and asked the students for the third time, "Is the jar full?" This time, the students giggled a bit and once again answered, "Yes, the jar is now full."

The professor finally reached underneath his desk one more time and brought up two bottles of beer. After pouring the two beers to the very top of the jar, he looked up and addressed the class, saying something I may be paraphrasing a bit:

> *The jar itself represents your life, and you can certainly have a full and happy life. The rocks represent the most important and most valuable things in your life. They are things like your health, your family, and your true friends. You need to guard them, because they are precious, and you need to place them in your life first. The pebbles are also important. They represent things like your schooling, your job, your house, your investments, your hobbies, and your car perhaps. Yes, the pebbles are important, but they are smaller in real value than the rocks, so they need to be placed in your life after the rocks are secure inside your life.*
>
> *As for the sand, it simply represents all that other stuff that just happens in life. Stuff that is certainly less important in the grand scheme of things. These can be described as minor, and they're just too many to count. All that stuff that the sand represents is far less valuable than the rocks and pebbles, so you have to be on guard when they sneak into your life, whether you like it or not. The most important thing to understand is that if you try to put all these elements in your life in a different sequence, you'll find that they just won't fit.*

The professor then went on to point out the moral of the story, which is the following:

> *After you have filled your life with the most important things first, and your life is full of health, family, friends, house, job, car, hobbies, and all the other stuff, there is always room for a couple of beers.*

Reflection Questions for Chapter 3:

1. Can you think of a time when you deliberately avoided a critical step during a project, thinking it would save you time?

2. What was the damage incurred in terms of time, energy, and money?

4

WIRING DIAGRAMS AND SHOT GLASSES

There is no question, at least not in my mind, that the United States of America is one of the most amazing countries on earth. For better or worse, its history is unlike any other. People from all walks of life, from all over the world, continue to sacrifice and try to escape the hardships and tyranny of the dictatorships they face in their home countries, while striving to arrive and take refuge in the US. They're all hoping for a better future for themselves and their families. They're all looking forward to living in the land of opportunity. I can certainly relate and can also attest that I am very fortunate to have recently become a US citizen myself.

As amazing as it happens to be, the US is not perfect by any stretch of the imagination. The journey of the United States as a country from its inception to where we are today has certainly been bumpy, with lots of hills and valleys, to say the least. Still, we should all be able to agree that there is something very special about it, as it continues to draw people toward the ideas from which America was born.

There are countless books, articles, lessons learned, and other opinions about this country, all of which matter. The events that took place along the way are important for our understanding of how we got here as a nation. We should all take the time to review and appreciate our country's history. Moving forward from here is perhaps even more important.

I mentioned earlier the well-known phrase written in the July 4, 1776 Declaration of Independence, which states that everyone has the God-given, unalienable right to *life, liberty, and the pursuit of happiness.* Imagine that. The US government was set up to protect the life of its citizens while the people are free to pursue the things that make them happy. This Declaration of Independence, along with its constitution and amendments, makes the United States unique among all the countries on earth.

Considering where we are today as a whole, I happen to be in the camp of the former president of the United States, Ronald Reagan, who emphasized that "America is a shining city upon a hill whose beacon light guides freedom-loving people everywhere." Despite all the bumps and bruises along the way, the US still provides hope to others who want to be a part of it. People from all over the globe continue to want to come here. People with diverse backgrounds and unique ways of thinking want to contribute their ideas, hoping for the opportunity to improve their lives.

Having said all that as an introduction to this chapter, I want to tell you about this guy who visited a nearby zoo on a beautiful sunny day. He ended up near a group of people who had all gathered to watch a bear sitting down making some whining sounds every thirty seconds or so. As everyone was watching the whining bear with curiosity, this guy asked the zookeeper if he had any idea as to why it was whining. Everyone thought that the bear was hurt somehow or likely in some pain. The zookeeper promptly replied that the bear was sitting on a rough board that had a nail in it. *Ouch!!* "So why doesn't the bear just get off the nail?" asked the guy. The zookeeper smirked a bit and replied, "Because it only hurts him enough to whine about it, not enough for him to move."

I'm not sure where I heard this whining-bear-at-the-zoo story, nor am I sure whether it's true or false. I wanted to respectfully point out that when you look among the general population around the globe, there seem to be a lot of folks—undoubtedly in pain—complaining about their situation. Once again, I'm not suggesting that their pain isn't real; I'm only proposing that their situation might improve if they would just consider doing something different from what has obviously not been working.

Perhaps try a different thinking approach. Perhaps consider a thorough review of the circumstances. Perhaps ask for guidance or read to gain the education needed. Perhaps the company you keep is limiting your growth potential. Perhaps reducing the complaining is easier said than done, but I will always be an advocate for investing in yourself. This gradual, continuous self-improvement will pay dividends to you and your circle of influence for a lifetime.

Have you ever met someone who is constantly reminding you and everyone else how bad their situation is, even though you know that they could help themselves? Have you noticed how some individuals seem to draw the oxygen right out of a room when they enter and begin speaking? Have you experienced your energy draining right out of your body while in someone's presence? You immediately feel the need to look around for the nearest exit before you pass out. Seriously, there are negative people everywhere who certainly don't want to hear that they may be the ones responsible for the dark clouds following them around everywhere.

I'll be the first to admit that I've had my brief occasions of venting, as I'm sure we all have. I've mentioned it many times at work or with family and friends that, in my humble opinion, it's our personal *onboard computer wiring* that makes us do what we do—or what we don't do. Essentially, we're all wired differently, and that's a good thing. We generate ideas and do things in various ways for various reasons based on our unique upbringing, education, living environment, travel exposure, and various other factors.

It's our individual culture. It's the people we spend time with in our immediate circle. It's our work. It's the programs and news we're exposed to on TV. It's the books we've read. It's the places we visited. It's our personal experiences, both good and bad. We all tend to think, speak, and do things according to our individual *wiring diagram*.

Because we each come from different backgrounds with different customs, different experiences, different reference points, and different personalities, we're all wired differently from each other. It's not wrong; it's just different. It's part of what makes each of us a one-of-a-kind masterpiece. It's our personal wiring diagram that is either fixed and rigid, or is constantly adjusted, fine-tuned, and upgraded according to how we see and understand things.

What exactly are those hot buttons that make some people draw a line in the sand and declare, "That's enough! I'm fed up and I'm doing something about it"? What is it that moves one person to take immediate action while another person completely ignores the same dire circumstances they find themselves in? Yes, life can be chaotic at times, but how do some people manage things in a relatively controlled manner while others appear to be stressed out all the time? Why do some people appear to have their act together while so many others seem to be spinning in circles or stuck in a rut getting absolutely nowhere? I have to believe that most people have heard of the expression, "Doing the same thing but expecting different results is the definition of insanity."

Henry Ford once said, "If you think you can, or if you think you can't, you're right." That pretty much spells it out. Your personal wiring causes you to think the way you do. It causes you to choose what you choose and to believe what you believe to be either true or false. Your personal wiring may even convince you that your outlook on life has no need of any enhancements at all. Your attitude is just fine, you may reason. You've got it all figured out. You're not negative, it's just all this bad luck that keeps following you everywhere.

You could certainly decide to shut down and conclude that you don't need any suggestions from anyone. Hey, it's a free country. Or you may choose to consider that there are other possibilities and your situation can improve if you were to decide to study the problem a bit. It's totally up to you which path you take. You're in charge, after all. Perhaps there are options by which you can learn something you didn't know before. Maybe it's worth looking into it. Maybe you will realize that you can make a positive difference. Maybe you will wish that you had looked into it earlier.

The good news, again, in my humble opinion, is that wiring diagrams can be adjusted and enhanced if you allow yourself to recognize what needs to be updated. Once that recognition happens, you must also be willing to go through a sort of reprogramming. It's learning what you didn't know that reprograms your onboard wiring. Every new piece of information gained adds a higher level of understanding. Your subsequent wiring diagram will then cause you to create new thoughts, new words, and new behaviors that are at a higher, more informed level than before. There is a pretty good chance that this updated wiring diagram will, in turn, lead you toward gradual resolutions and ultimately a better future.

This brings us to what I have coined as the *shot-glass capacity* analogy. Imagine a typical one-ounce shot glass. It has a limited capacity; it can hold only one ounce of liquid. If you fill it to the very top, and then try to pour anything else into it, all that extra stuff will simply overflow, spill on the outside, and be wasted. If you need a container to hold anything greater than one ounce of liquid, you have to be willing to get a larger glass or a mug or a bucket or a barrel or, well, you get the idea.

The shot glass observation helps us visualize the relatively small capacity analogous to our personal onboard computer—our brain—since we were born. As time passes and we grow older, we continue to fill the shot glass with information until it is full. I've heard it said that during the first few months of a baby's life, it is somewhat like a puppy. Yes, the baby needs a lot more care during this time and long afterward, but both the baby and the puppy pretty much just cry, crawl, eat, sleep, and poop for the first few months of their lives.

The remarkable thing is that the baby continues to learn new things long after the first few months. Unlike the puppy, the baby begins learning to talk and reason and evaluate and express new ideas. The shot glass—the infant's storage capacity—continues to fill up as new information is being absorbed during infancy and subsequently as a child. Then come the challenging adolescent years, then hopefully the development of a healthy adult.

This is where it begins to be a bit trickier, as the adult is free to choose and make decisions. Somewhere along the line, as a result of many factors, the adult may end up in a predicament that causes them pain. This is when the adult can make the choice to get a bigger glass—an increase of storage capacity—in order to gain additional understanding of the problem causing the pain. This choice to get a bigger glass is the adult's willingness to learn something new.

If anyone tries to teach something new to the adult who is in pain, but the person isn't willing to learn, then in effect the person isn't willing to increase the size of their glass. Their capacity to understand their predicament is limited by refusing to learn something new. Their pain and the complaining will likely continue. Any attempt by the teacher to pour the new information into the adult's limited-capacity shot glass will simply spill over on the outside and be wasted.

Albert Einstein has been quoted as saying, "We cannot solve our problems with the same level of thinking that created them." There must be a willingness on the adult's part to learn something new, thereby creating some new capacity where the information can be stored and used. It is through this new information that our wiring diagrams are adjusted over time to create new thoughts, new words, and new actions toward resolution of our problems.

We all have the ability to learn, and we ought to embrace it for self-improvement. I consider myself a lifelong learner. I've concluded some time ago that I'm naturally curious about why things are the way they are. I suppose I want to be better equipped for the unexpected by being as prepared as possible. Benjamin Franklin once said that "an investment in knowledge pays the best interest."

So, there you have it. In a nutshell, this is part of what prompted me to write this book. *It's my wiring.* I want to offer suggestions of how you can achieve better results in many aspects of life. I want to help. I want to share with you some of the knowledge I have gained from my experiences with the hope that you will benefit from them. I want to help you arrive at the conviction, confidence, and comfort that can be gained from knowing that you've got what it takes to improve every area of your life. That's why later in this book I'm going to share with you the Believe-Observe-Will improvement process that worked for me.

Reflection Questions for Chapter 4:

1. Can you think of anyone who claims to be open-minded yet displays little evidence of any upgrade to their own wiring diagram?

2. Can you describe a situation when the capacity of your shot glass was increased?

5
THE GREATEST ATTRIBUTES

I joke about it now, but there was a time when I thought that I had it all figured out. Maybe you did too. Maybe you still do. There are a few things I know to be true as I write this, but thinking that I've got it all figured out is no longer one of them. I have been humbled many times since then, and I'm glad it happened that way. That original thought has completely faded away from the radar screen of my convictions. In retrospect, I know that it was a foolish thought to begin with, and now it only exists in my not-too-distant past.

Whatever was going on in my mind during that time, I recall it was just after the December 1980 car accident I was in where my little sister died. She was eighteen, and I was twenty-one. My way of thinking from that point forward was certainly affected, as I couldn't make much sense of why I survived that day and she didn't. Even though I was missing her dearly, I kept myself preoccupied by staying busy on purpose. On a side note, I dedicated a chapter to her in my first book, as she continues to provide inspiration and hope. Her name was Rodica.

After the accident, I recall thinking that I would eventually finish school, get a good job, get married, have a family one day, and live in a nice neighborhood. I suppose I wanted the proverbial

American dream a lot of people are still striving for. I know that I have also used the expression "I want it all" a few times in my life. Maybe you've expressed a similar sentiment. I suppose there is nothing wrong with striving for a higher standard, but thinking that I knew how that would all unfold was certainly a mistake on my part. Did I mention that I was humbled along the way?

I was about to start my second year in university for mechanical engineering. I needed to apply for special permission from the dean of engineering because I had failed one class in my first year, and I also had to repeat a couple of courses for which I got D's. This was uncharted territory for me. I needed to fill out an application requesting an overload to the second-year course curriculum. I needed to repeat the three courses from my first year, and I wanted to add them to the full second-year course load.

Throughout my high school years, I didn't really struggle with any subject except history, and I had very good grades for the most part while managing playing sports and getting involved in other activities. I found university a lot more intense, but I actually enjoyed the math and science subjects in the engineering program. Although I had other distractions during that time, I take full responsibility for all the outcomes. The truth is that I didn't focus as much as I needed to during my first year in university, thus, the poor grades.

I recall walking into the dean's office with the course-overload application in my hand, as he greeted me and asked me to have a seat so we could talk. His office was somewhere on the tenth floor of the math building. He started by asking me why I wanted to apply for the course overload because his initial opinion was that I would find it very difficult. I explained that I had never failed any course previously, and I was committed to work harder in the second year so I could catch up. I went on to say that I also wanted to finish the four-year engineering program with the class I had started with. There was certainly my pride working overtime in the background.

The dean emphasized that the second-year curriculum was much more difficult than the first and that I needed help. He tried to impress on me that I would be much better off to *reduce* my second-year course load significantly, while adding the three mandatory courses I needed to repeat from the first year. His advice was for me to carry a reduced overall course load for the following four years. Essentially, he suggested that I pace myself with fewer courses going forward, thus completing the mechanical engineering program in a total of five years instead of four.

I certainly wasn't prepared to consider what the dean had just said, nor did I honestly want to hear it. I respectfully replied by asking if it was up to his discretion whether he would sign my application, or if it would ultimately be up to me. This is where his words set me back a bit as he replied, "You filling out this course-overload application is like you volunteering to step onto the windowsill of this office. Asking me to sign it is like asking me to push you over the edge. I have given you my best advice, but it is ultimately your decision."

Wow!! I thought the analogy was a bit extreme, but it was certainly memorable. After sitting back in my chair for a moment, I looked up and quietly asked him to sign my application. I ended up walking out of his office, still in a bit of shock, but with my application signed. I was certainly warned, but I had gotten what I wanted. Little did I realize at the time that what I wanted was definitely not what I needed. As you might have guessed by now, I should have listened to the dean.

After the dust settled from the mess I created for myself during the chaotic second year, I ended up finishing up my mechanical engineering program in a total of five years, just as the dean had originally advised. I ate some humble pie for the remainder of my schooling. I certainly made it harder for myself, and it didn't have to be that way.

Humility and *honesty* are at the top of the list of the greatest attributes one can turn to when attempting to improve the situation they're in. It all starts here. The lack of understanding in this area will manifest itself over and over in your life until the painful lesson is learned. We can certainly learn from our own experiences, and we can also learn from those of others. The main point is to take the time and appreciate the immeasurable value of these two attributes.

I'd say that we all struggle to some degree with this humility and honesty apprenticeship program. Perhaps it's in our nature to appear to others as though we've got our act together, as we look for things we want to hear, rather than those things we need to hear. I'm hopeful we can all agree that we need to continuously humble ourselves and acknowledge the truth first, even if it hurts, in order to have a better chance for lasting solutions to our problems.

When I look back and reflect, I can come up with a few more instances when I should have humbled myself first. I should have taken a deep breath, and I should have taken full responsibility for the position I found myself in at that time. It was my problem, and, in retrospect, I could have dealt with it in a different way. Better yet, I should have avoided it altogether. The moral of the story is pretty much the same. Approaching a problem with humility and honesty is an excellent place to start from. When we're in any kind of pain, but we're only looking for shortcuts, we're likely setting ourselves up for bigger problems.

Among the many lessons along the way, I have learned that I can only do my part. I have also learned that I cannot help anyone who refuses to humble themselves and acknowledge the truth or reality of their own situation. We each have to want to help ourselves, and it all starts with a humble and honest heart. When that happens, I have found that many other doors will open. We may not be able to do everything all at once, but we certainly can, and should, do what is within our ability at every opportunity possible for as long as it may take.

Other positive attributes that come to mind for us all to lean on are *love, patience, persistence, integrity, character, accountability, gratitude, peace, kindness, compassion,* and *self-control.* All of these can help guide us toward a better understanding of the problems we each face, and subsequently toward improvements.

Reflection Questions for Chapter 5:

1. What situation stands out in your mind when you were personally humbled?

2. Can you describe a time in your life or someone else's life when the truth eventually came out?

6

THE GREATEST ADVERSARIES

In spite of my personal view that the United States of America is one of the greatest countries that someone can be a part of, something very disturbing seems to be going on, not just here in the US, but literally around the entire world these days. The signs are everywhere; they're overwhelming. There is a growing sense of despair among people from all walks of life, with no sign of abating anytime soon. With global social media in full swing, there is certainly no shortage of up-to-date news stories as well as opinions as to why this is happening.

- Drug abuse is on the rise, and it is lowering the average American life expectancy.
- Suicide rates in the US have increased substantially during the past two decades.
- Homelessness and bankruptcies, especially among seniors, are increasing rapidly.
- An increasing number of seniors are either remaining in or reentering the work force due to lack of savings.
- A record number of young people are not working at all.

- Student debt is at an all-time high, and defaults on the loans are approaching 100,000 per month.
- About 75% of American parents are still supporting their adult children.
- About 20% of Americans have more credit card debt than savings for their future.
- Despite additional hours worked, millions of Americans still struggle to make ends meet.
- Young men and women are flocking toward extreme political views.
- Anger, resentment, and violence are on the rise.
- People are fearful and are being hassled in public spaces as well as outside their own homes for their political affiliation.

So, what is really going on? What underlies all these problems? According to some "experts," they would suggest that the rising tension in this country is caused by inequality, privilege, low wages, rising housing costs, politicians, taxes, large banks and corporations, the growing gap between the rich and poor, jobs moving overseas, Civil War statues from a hundred years ago, or a combination of some or all of the above. People are dealing with a lot of pain, and there is a growing sense of unrest while everyone is searching for some much-needed relief.

Pride and *procrastination*, in my humble opinion, are at the top of the list of the greatest adversaries standing in the way of our ability to move forward toward resolution of many problems we all face in life. They are both huge stumbling blocks, but they don't have to remain that way. As with anything else, we need to learn about them to understand the steps we need to take to minimize them. To simply state part of the problem a different way, we obviously cannot postpone taking necessary action any longer. When I include the word *pride* on the list of adversaries, I'm referring to the boastful and bragging kind of pride. It's the puffing-up-the-chest kind, not the taking-pride-in-one's-work kind.

Although we can all see that there are many larger-scale problems around us, I would venture to guess that most of us are busy dealing with our own personal ecosystem of issues, or at least we should be. We all have our opinions as to how things got to this seemingly desperate state in our country, as well as opinions about what can be done about them. We also can, and certainly should, participate in the voting process that was established so that we could voice our opinions. Like in any other government, however, the changes needed will certainly take time.

As for the personal predicaments we're each dealing with daily, perhaps we can focus more of our attention on what it takes to make positive improvements in the areas closer to home. We'll have to take it one day at a time, and we'll have to stay with it. We'll have to go through the ups and downs, and we'll have to be patient, yet persistent. As the saying goes, Rome wasn't built in a day, but I have to believe someone decided to start building Rome at some point, and they stuck with it until it was built.

So what's the holdup? What is preventing us from taking a closer look in our own backyard? What are the roadblocks to understanding how we can each improve our personal situation, as well as prioritize the measures we should implement first? Why do a lot of people spend time pointing out deficiencies in others while not looking in the mirror first and helping themselves? Should we start looking into it today or should we wait until tomorrow?

If you had a bad cold and went to the drugstore, you would find all kinds of medications on the shelves, some boasting fast-acting relief and others claiming long-lasting relief. It may sound funny, but you're put in the position of deciding whether you'd like to buy the medication that gives you relief from your cold right away, or perhaps you'd like to consider buying the medication that will make you feel better for a longer period of time. So, let's see, do you want to feel better now or later? It's possible I missed it when I looked on the shelves of the drugstore, but maybe there can be only one medication to help you feel better now *and* later. I suspect company sales had a lot to do with why I didn't find it.

Procrastination is one of the greatest adversaries we each face when it comes to achieving progress. I've heard it said that the word *tomorrow* is the most debilitating word in the English language. Procrastination is being stuck in a perpetual state of delays, and I'll be the first to admit that avoiding that state takes some practice. We all have to be aware of its negative impact and also recognize when it's creeping up on us unexpectedly. I mean, everyone has the right to put things off, but it seems that some people really abuse the privilege.

Perhaps it is human nature to keep postponing fixes until there is an absolute emergency, but for the most part, it's not a good idea. I have yet to hear someone say, "Here's the plan: We will delay all research into the improvements needed in our lives because things are still hanging in there by a thread, and there's no reason to overreact or move too soon." Of course, nobody says that, but in reality, that seems to be exactly what's going on. Those same people who have the clouds of bad luck following them everywhere have really perfected the art of procrastination. They have apparently practiced it a lot.

Every day is a new opportunity to learn something that will improve your situation. How you spend your spare time matters when it comes to how quickly you notice the improvements you desire. We all need to be willing to swallow our pride and admit the condition we're in. We all need to be willing to get educated by digging and researching for relevant information and answers to each of our personal dilemmas. In essence, we're getting a bigger glass while upgrading our wiring diagram at the same time. We will all be much better prepared to fix our own problems and perhaps may avoid the emergency altogether.

The truth is that we're all flawed because we're human. We tend to say we want to know the truth, but we don't necessarily want to hear it in its raw, unadulterated form. If things are not going well, the truth sounds a bit harsh and certainly gloomy. We tend to minimize or mask the problem. We may even bury our heads in the sand and pretend it doesn't exist. We tend to listen for things we *want* to hear, rather than for the things we *need* to hear. As a result of some of these flaws, we can get fooled into thinking that things aren't really that bad. We make excuses, we complain, and we blame others instead of taking ownership of our situation.

Although pride and procrastination are at the top of my list of greatest adversaries, there are certainly others that can be stumbling blocks on the road to recovery. Some of those that come to mind are *doubt, depravity, deception, vanity, immorality, indifference, ignorance, entitlement, hostility,* and *aggression*. Entire novels can be written about each of these subjects. I've just briefly mentioned them here because we all need to be aware of them and guard ourselves against them so that we avoid falling into their traps.

The expression, "The truth shall set you free" is important to remember. All the adversaries listed can blind us and oppress us from the freedom that truth can unleash. On the other hand, an honest, thorough review and admission of where you are can help start the improvement process. Facing the reality of your situation matters, as it's one of the first steps toward recovery. This may be obvious, but it's certainly worth stating that the sooner you face the truth, the sooner you can begin the healing process.

So, what do you think? Can you handle the truth? Are you ready to generate some immediate *and* lasting relief or would you prefer to postpone it for a while longer? Regardless of where your starting line is or how you got there, will you consider facing the truth so you can begin moving forward, or will you continue to allow your pride to stand in the way? I've heard it said that an excuse is nothing but the skin of a reason stuffed with a lie. If you were thirsty and someone were to bring you to a location with some cool, fresh water, would you be willing to take a drink? Horse, meet water.

The current generation doesn't seem to be doing a very good job of leaving their kids and grandchildren better off than they are. The subject of money being scarce continues to come up. Most people cannot, or will not, distinguish the difference between a *want* and a *need*, thus continuing to live way beyond their realistic means. They're either purposely ignoring the signs or they're too proud to admit that they're clueless about how disastrous this is for their future as they get older.

A young man was being interviewed after winning first place and a very large sum of money. The reporter began by asking him what he would do with his winnings. The young man smiled and calmly explained that he used to work in his dad's pawn shop growing up. Although he earned a very modest wage during those early years, he had learned the power of saving and investing and hard work early on in his life. He then went on to say that the most valuable lesson his dad gave him was to never forget that he was only one bad decision away from ending up on the other side of the counter. It certainly sounded like this young man learned the value of keeping pride and procrastination in check.

To put it mildly, a whole lot has been written on the subject of money. Debts can certainly be accumulated quickly as a result of only one bad decision, which can, in turn, cause a lifetime of misery. Taking the time to understand how money works and practicing sound money management principles will very likely ensure that you will never become a slave to money. Instead, you will learn and grasp the truth of the liberating power of making money serve you and your loved ones.

Like anything else, it will take time, and you must be willing to do it. You have to humble yourself by setting aside the pride, then focus on and investigate your personal predicaments right away by eliminating procrastination in order to discover the things you don't know. If you choose to do so, then in due time, you will no longer deal with the relentless stress of scarce funds, nor live near the edge of default. You will have invested in yourself, and it will pay you dividends for your entire lifetime, as well as benefiting future generations.

REFLECTION QUESTIONS FOR CHAPTER 6:

1. When was the last time you allowed your pride to get you in trouble?

2. What can you think of that caused you pain in some way because you didn't address it on time?

7
PRECIOUS COMMODITIES

Our planet Earth is quite the place, isn't it? There is nothing like it anywhere in the known universe, although I realize people are still looking. It is capable of sustaining life as we know it to exist. The earth is home to all of us human beings, as well as all living creatures everywhere. We get to walk and drive around on the solid surfaces, swim in the waters, and even use airplanes to fly through the air from one place to another. The fish and marine life pretty much live in the waters of the earth, while the birds can fly in the air for short periods of time before landing back on the surface to rest.

The paragraph above can be a simple way to describe the basics of the planet Earth to a very young child who may be curious and ask questions about it. That's what all kids do. They wonder and ask questions and soak up information the way a dry sponge quickly absorbs water. No doubt there are other ways to answer the child's question. For the purpose of this chapter, I wanted to begin with the simplicity of the description in the first paragraph, and lead in to what makes our planet Earth even more remarkable. It is full of precious commodities.

A commodity can be generally described in the following three ways:

- *A reasonably exchangeable good or material, bought and sold as an article of commerce.*
- *A raw material or primary agricultural product that can be bought or sold.*
- *A useful or valuable thing.*

These commodities come in different types, with some examples listed below:

- *Metals—Gold, silver, platinum, and copper*
- *Energy—Crude oil, heating oil, natural gas, and gasoline*
- *Livestock and Meat—Pork, beef, and poultry*
- *Agricultural—Corn, wheat, rice, coffee, soybeans, cotton, cocoa, and sugar*

We all need commodities, as they are an important part of everyday life. They supply food, energy, and metals used in construction and other useful items like cars, kitchen appliances, and TVs. For the most part, all the people of the earth use commodities found on and under the earth's surface. Some countries are rich with some commodities, while other countries have a surplus of others. That's where trade and commerce take place among the nations across this unique planet.

If there is an extended drought somewhere, we can expect the cost of agricultural products to increase because there will be a smaller crop that year. If there is some unexpected freezing weather in Florida for a long period of time, we can expect the price of orange juice to go up. If there is an interruption in oil flow anywhere in the world for any reason, we can expect the cost of gasoline for our cars to go up. If there is a disease spreading among domestic animal farms, we can expect the cost of that meat product to go up.

The price we pay for each commodity is usually a function of the economic relationship between supply and demand. In general, when a commodity becomes scarcer, even temporarily, then we can expect to pay more for it. There are certainly other factors that affect the price we pay for the commodities we use. For example, the cost it takes to mine some metals out of the ground, the availability of equipment, how remote the locations are, shipping costs, and labor costs are all factored into the price we the consumers ultimately pay.

When it comes to commodities like metals and energy, we need to mine or extract them from beneath the earth's surface. Those are considered nonrenewable commodities because they cannot be readily replaced. Once things like oil or coal or natural gas are removed from beneath the earth's surface, they can be turned into useful fuels. Once these fuels are burned, then more commodities need to be extracted to create more of them. To some degree, we can recycle metals like steel and copper from demolition sites and scrapyards. We can reuse a lot of those metals without needing much more. However, as the world population increases, more construction ramps up to meet the needs of the additional people. As a result, more new commodities need to be extracted over and above those being recycled.

When it comes to meat and agricultural products, farmers all over the globe have figured out ways to keep up with the increased need for food products. Large crops that grow in the ground are replanted and harvested repeatedly, then shipped everywhere. Large facilities for fish, chicken, beef, and pork are constantly updated and maintained to provide the continuous supply of food for the population of the globe.

Notice the third definition of what a commodity is: *a useful or valuable thing*. Besides the metals, fuels, meats, and agricultural products mentioned above, what else can we consider to be a useful and valuable thing? Even if you had all the money in the world, and you could buy lots of precious metals and jewels and houses and all kinds of other stuff, what could you never buy more of? The amazing thing about this most precious commodity is that there is a limited supply of it, yet it is available to all of us regardless of financial status. Sadly, not everyone takes full advantage of it to help resolve their problems.

Time. It's the most precious commodity of all. Nobody on the planet can produce any more of it, nobody can purchase any of it with any amount of money, yet the exact same amount of time available in a day is accessible to everyone. Every second of every minute of every hour of every day of your life will never be recovered, once the calendar flips to the next day. Once time is spent, it's gone forever. How each person uses their allotted time makes all the difference.

You will never get today back, so how you spend your day matters more than you realize. If you're constantly feeling like *there isn't enough time in a day*, then it would make sense to stop and examine the details of your days, so you get a full understanding of how they are used up. If you have the chance to improve your life all day today, and you don't take advantage of that opportunity, you have just wasted one day of your most precious commodity. Out of the remaining days available to you, you now have one day less.

Right about now, someone might be quick to point out that we may choose to spend a day with friends and family, so how could that be a waste of a day? Of course, spending a day with friends and family would be a great way to use it. That would have been a day in which you invested in your relationship. That would certainly not have been a waste of a day.

No doubt you've heard the expression, "Time is money." The way we spend our time can be considered in two basic ways. Just to keep it simple, we either *invest* our time, or we *waste* our time. It's no surprise that when you talk to people about their lifestyles, the ones who believe this expression tend to be the busiest people, as they take advantage of most of their available time, while the people who think of it as nothing more than a mere expression are the people who tend to be the least busy at anything productive, thus wasting a lot of their available time.

Shortly after I had started my working career, the company I was working for set up a seminar for us on time management. It was an educational course given so we could gain a better understanding of the value of time. It was certainly intended to help us be more productive throughout the workday. It was an excellent course. I still remember the instructor reminding us that what we were learning in the class would be beneficial to the company we worked for as well as for our personal lives outside of work.

I can still hear her emphasize how spending our time can be thought of in terms of *deposits* and *withdrawals*. We either spend our time making deposits into ourselves and into others around us, or we make withdrawals from ourselves and from others. *Making deposits means we invest our time. Making withdrawals means we waste our time.*

Deposits, for the most part, pay interest and dividends. Deposits tend to advance progress and resolve problems. Withdrawals reduce the available capital we have to work with. They typically increase our daily problems. When we use time to deposit, we build. When we use time to make withdrawals, we diminish. It's funny how I still recall one example the instructor gave us. As an illustration, she said that if we take the time to compliment our spouse, we make a deposit in our relationship. If we waste time on criticizing our spouse, it could turn out to be a very costly withdrawal.

I've heard it said that all things come to those who wait. What a crippling myth this is. So should we all just simply wait around for things to somehow come our way? Sure, great idea. Let's just all hang out for a while and see what happens. I would venture to guess that some people think this expression was intended to exalt the virtue of patience, or something like that.

Who started this nonsense anyway, and why do so many people feel so empowered by saying it, as if to explain their reason for not taking any positive action? According to Wikipedia, apparently

Violet Fane can be credited with having said this phrase back in 1892, although it was in the larger context of a poem she wrote. Most people likely don't know that there is a slightly different version of the phrase too. This other version is believed to have been expressed by Abraham Lincoln as "Things may come to those who wait, but only the things left by those who hustle." You can choose for yourself which version fits you better.

Time sure flies, and it can slip right through our fingers practically without detection. There is certainly a time for everything, with tons of literature already written about it everywhere we look. There are even songs written about it. Planting a seed or an idea in due season produces a harvest for you to enjoy later. Planting nothing produces nothing but emptiness and scarcity. I chose to write this book because I believed it would be worthy of my time. I wanted to take the time to communicate a process that has helped me move forward from the starting line of my personal predicament to where I am today.

Over the years, I have tried to make the most of my spare time by learning more about the issues I was dealing with. I have read books, I have asked questions, I researched, I have signed up for countless free webinars, and I have personally attended classes and live seminars as well. I have also learned to take advantage of the time spent in my car while driving to work. I listened to useful and relevant educational materials on topics like relationships, history, the nature of man, independent thinking, investing, money, and God, not necessarily in that order.

Everyone needs to juggle work time, family time, and fun and relaxation time. All these times are important, and we all need to be mindful to keep them in balance. The goal is to identify, recognize, and ultimately *fully utilize* our available time and not waste it.

Planting an idea for improvement into our minds and then not taking the time to expand on it and gain understanding of how to implement that thought is a waste of a good idea. Some ideas are quick to execute, while others may take more time. Similarly, planting a small seed of a tree without watering it allows the seed to wither away. It will take continuous nurturing for some time before the small seed begins to grow roots so it can become a self-sufficient, mature, freestanding, solid tree.

We can all agree that there is always room for improvement, so this is not a one-size-fits-all or a one-time thing we do. Perhaps we can also agree that we should be actively pursuing ways to improve our lives and thus continuously be working on it. Investing our most precious commodity—time—in others can also take us on an emotional rollercoaster. It's the greatest gift we can give to someone as we essentially give away a portion of our lives that we can never get back.

I'm hopeful that the material I am covering in this book is making an investment, a deposit, in those who spend their time reading it. I'm hopeful that you will find it useful so that it causes you to take action toward improving your life. I'm hopeful that the time you've invested in it already will pay you dividends. And I'm hopeful it will help you right away, as well as in the long run. Of course, as we both know, only time will tell.

Reflection Questions for Chapter 7:

1. Name the activities that take up the majority of your spare time.

2. Which of those activities are helping you gain understanding to resolve your problems, and which activities are not helping?

8
OXYGEN MASKS

So you get on a plane and just before takeoff, the flight attendants try to get the passengers' attention for a routine preflight briefing. They go through a series of possible emergency procedures for the awareness of everyone on board. If you have ever flown, you've seen the drill. Sure, they have to tell us all these things from a legal point of view, but the information is for everyone's own good. The intention is to better prepare the passengers to know what to do in case of unexpected emergencies throughout the flight.

At some point during this safety presentation, we hear, "Put on your own oxygen mask first, before assisting others." This phrase certainly comes across as a sort of instruction with a hint of a command. I don't recall any flight attendant ever prefacing that statement with something like, "We suggest . . ." or "We prefer . . ." or "It is highly recommended that . . ." They are telling us that in the event of an emergency, we each need to do our very best to put on our own mask first. We can then look around and assist others who may be having difficulty with their own mask, or with anything else for that matter.

This seems to make sense, since you need to have oxygen to be conscious, thus being able to perhaps help others. I hope I never get to experience any airplane emergency procedure in real life, but the emergency presentation is a good reminder of what to do. I also trust that the airlines have researched the effectiveness of their instructions. I also have to believe that they likely adjusted and improved them over time. The reasoning for having to put on my own oxygen mask first sounds right, so I'll just take their word for it.

    A real-life example that comes to mind with respect to dealing with an unforeseen emergency happened at my place of work many years ago. A maintenance worker went down a ladder into a large, open pit to investigate the reason for a conveyor belt not working. A few minutes later, the foreman went to check on the progress, only to find that the maintenance worker was collapsed on the ground next to the conveyor tail drum. Not knowing what happened, the foreman called on the radio for a nurse as well as other backup. As soon as the nurse arrived on the scene, they both quickly made their way down the ladder to help the motionless maintenance worker at the bottom of the pit.

    Shortly thereafter, both the foreman and the nurse also collapsed next to the maintenance worker. By this time, other personnel had arrived at the top of the pit, with most individuals not really being able to process what was taking place right in front of their eyes. Everyone seemed to have that puzzled look of helplessness watching all three bodies now lying next to each other, motionless. Someone then quickly assessed that carbon monoxide had to have been trapped at the bottom of the pit, and this may have caused all three people to go unconscious.

    Fortunately, this incident had a happy ending. As it turned out, another foreman who had arrived at the scene felt strong enough, and also felt compelled to jump into action. Armed with the new information of the potential hazard, he immediately decided to hold his breath while descending quickly into the pit. No doubt the adrenaline boosted his energy as he was able to carry up one person at a time on his shoulder. With additional assistance, each person was retrieved out of the deadly pit environment to safety. This all took place while someone else got the emergency oxygen masks for those who were temporarily overcome. With fresh air being introduced in the area and a little time spent by the emergency crew, it turned out that everyone was OK.

The follow-up review and investigation of that incident led to some engineering improvements, as well as many training sessions across the entire plant. Everyone was expected to learn from the unfortunate experience and become aware of the hazards in the area, as well as the preparations needed for any possible recurrence. One of the main themes of the safety training was the need to put on the oxygen mask first, before assisting others.

The concept is the same for other emergencies, such as someone who cannot swim falling into a deep pool or a lake. It's probably human nature to want to jump in to save the person from drowning. However, grabbing a nearby flotation device, a life jacket, or a rescue pole might help more than quickly jumping into danger, even with your best intentions.

It's also true that the person who didn't know how to swim could have been wearing a life jacket when on a boat or near open water. Regardless, whether it's putting on your oxygen mask first in case of an emergency, or putting on your life jacket before jumping into the water to save someone else, the main message is the same. If you are better prepared ahead of time, you will be in a better position to survive an emergency as well as to help others do the same.

We have only briefly touched on two types of life-threatening emergencies in which preparation might have helped prevent the emergency altogether. There are all kinds of other unexpected situations that can develop quickly right out of left field. Many of them have to do with money. As you are surely aware, this is one of the main sources of anxiety for many people. People don't seem to have enough money and are having a lot of difficulty making ends meet.

There are very disturbing statistics when it comes to rising personal debt in America, and financial emergencies simply add to the already growing debt problem. A person's financial health can quickly spiral out of control, making all kinds of other unpleasant scenarios surface as well. A lot of people are only a minor setback away from not being able to pay something they owe. Their financial runway, so to speak, is getting shorter and shorter.

Debt, in general terms, can be described as money that is owed. It is essentially a note that is signed by the borrower who is promising the lender to pay back the borrowed money along with some interest. What is causing so many people to borrow so much money these days? Why do they get into so much debt? Why do banks, credit card companies, and other financial institutions, along with car companies and retail stores, continue to lend money to people who can barely keep their heads above water?

Former US President Andrew Jackson hated being in debt. It was written that he viewed debt as a sort of moral failing. Jackson thought that if someone was in debt, then that person was totally dependent on his creditors and had essentially lost his independence. Because of his strong personal views on debt, he extended those principles of fiscal responsibility to the entire country he felt responsible for.

For the first time ever, in early 1835, Andrew Jackson's persistence brought the US to the point of being debt-free. The spending was cut to such a point that all national outstanding debt was paid. For the first time in US history, the spending of the US government was pretty much in line with the revenue coming in. Unfortunately, the US debt-free status only lasted for a little more than a year. Fast-forward to where we are today: the US national deficit is currently approximately $22 trillion. It's hard to predict where this is all going for us as a nation, but intuitively, it just doesn't seem likely to end well.

It's also hard to wrap your mind around these numbers. This may be too simplistic, but just try to imagine our country having a 22-trillion-dollar invoice it is required to pay. We, as a nation, are in debt and therefore owe $22 T. Just to spell it out, each trillion dollars is 1,000 billion dollars. And each billion dollars is 1,000 million dollars. And we all have a pretty good idea that only *one* million dollars is a lot of money. So there you go. Our country is in debt, like . . . A WHOLE LOT.

Bringing this debt conversation back down to earth a bit, I simply wanted to point out that when entire nations are in debt, they essentially turn on the money-printing press and just make more, seemingly out of thin air. Without getting into the effect of all that, I would simply suggest looking up for yourself some historical facts about countries that have continued to print more money to get out of debt. Go ahead and see for yourself the consequences of those practices and form your own opinion of this practice. Then, consider why the price of everything continues to go up.

When it comes to our individual debt, it's a whole different story. We regular folks are expected to pay our debt. We're expected to not spend more than we earn. We're expected to be fiscally responsible. We don't have a money-printing press. Our bills don't just disappear on their own. If you're behind on payments for your bills, you get repeated calls from collection agencies. You get reminders, and the bills get bigger because of the added interest. It's a suffocating and vicious cycle.

This is a good place to point out that being in *manageable debt* is one thing. On the other hand, being in debt *over your head* is overwhelming for anyone and will eventually drown you if you don't react fast enough with extreme measures. Unmanageable debt is like a malignant disease; it will spread like wildfire into every part of your life. You begin to lie to yourself and others. You take more risks. You may even do things that are unlawful. You take on even more debt as you increase your credit limit, wrongly thinking that you can handle it. You get deceived into thinking that you can afford more. Your credit score will plunge, and you will be charged higher interest rates.

All this increasing debt will continue to gnaw at your soul. You will get the feeling that your life is unraveling right before your eyes and you have no control over what's going on. You will become desperate and feel powerless and hopeless. You're no longer free. You're in financial bondage, held captive by your unmanageable growing debt.

I continue to maintain that hopelessness comes from a lack of understanding of any subject. I mean, you just don't know what you don't know. If you have knowledge and understanding, then you're in a better position to make improvements and also avoid the problem going forward. Gaining understanding of the problem is the beginning of the solution.

If you *put on the financial oxygen mask*, you will be taking the first step to breathing easier as the fresh new oxygen of financial knowledge helps you think clearly. Your financial eyes will be opened to the reality of your predicament. If you *put on the financial life jacket*, you will have a chance at staying afloat and not drowning in debt. Even though your debt won't just disappear right away, your financial IQ will increase, and you will begin to understand how to manage and get out of it. Hope will return, and you will be in a better position to take the baby steps needed to keep your head above the sea of debt you may be in.

To be able to live comfortably in society at large, you have to know about how money works. Invest the time it takes to learn for yourself. There is ample free information. The whole financial formula is really quite simple when you think about it. *Spend less than you earn, and wisely invest the difference.* I'll be the first to admit that it's easier said than done. I'm constantly learning, but I'm also happy to say that it gets easier over time. It's never too late to begin. I encourage you to look in the mirror and declare that you're worth the investment. If you want to help others, begin by putting on your oxygen mask first.

REFLECTION QUESTIONS FOR CHAPTER 8:

1. When considering areas for self-improvement, which area do you feel you most need help with?

   _____
   _____
   _____
   _____
   _____
   _____
   _____
   _____
   _____
   _____

2. If you were to consider putting on you own financial oxygen mask first, how many areas of your life would benefit?

   _____
   _____
   _____
   _____
   _____
   _____
   _____
   _____
   _____
   _____
   _____

9

THE B.O.W. IMPROVEMENT PROCESS

I have waited to include this B.O.W. improvement process chapter at this point in the book on purpose. The content of all the preceding chapters is what has helped me along the way. I want to emphasize that the sequence of the material presented in the previous chapters was taken into consideration to provide a flow for positive impact. This was all done with the sole purpose of helping you better understand my humble journey as preparation to delve into the process I have used to attain measurable relief from my personal predicament since the year 2000.

We've come a long way, and we've covered a lot up to this point. At times, some of the material may have seemed somewhat basic and obvious, yet many people continue to remain stuck near their personal starting line for many years. If, for whatever reason, you've skipped ahead to get to this point without having read the preceding chapters, then all I can do is encourage you to stop right here. I would respectfully suggest that you pick up and continue from the place where you left off, as the material is presented in this sequence by design.

If you have not yet read the ideas presented in the previous chapters, moving forward from here will not be as effective, as you will be shortchanged on the context. It's certainly not too late. I readily admit that I have skipped ahead in some books I've read in the past also, only to find out later that I missed out on some important things when I eventually went back to catch up. If this is you, then this may be one of those decision points where you are personally tested as well.

On the other hand, if you're at this point in the book with the background of all the information from the preceding chapters in your back pocket, then let's go through a quick bullet-point summary, as I also find that repetition is worthwhile for retention.

- Being aware of our own behavior and habits, as well as human nature in general, is important. Gaining understanding of the subjects we'd like to improve in is the foundation upon which practical solutions are built. The level of improvement in any area of your life will be in direct proportion to the level of understanding gained on that subject.
- We all have unexpected personal predicaments we're dealing with in our everyday lives. We may even have the scars from some of those past events. Remember that it's not what happens to us that matters as much as how we react to those unexpected events. It may be difficult to deal with them, but it's not impossible.
- Life is a marathon, and we need proper conditioning for the long run. Regardless of your personal starting line, preparation is paramount in order to navigate the ups and downs of life. Continue to better prepare by taking all opportunities to keep learning, so you're ready for any changing conditions.
- The sequence in which we learn and do things matters. There are no shortcuts, as lessons build on each other. We gain expertise at something through mastering a series of sequential, gradual steps. Each step, in the proper sequence,

takes some time to learn. It may seem difficult or feel uncomfortable at first, but each conquered step helps us gain confidence as we begin to see improvements. This encourages us to keep climbing higher as we do so with greater ease.
- We all think differently because we're each wired in a unique way. Gain understanding of what makes you tick, and how you tick, and what gets you ticked off. Be willing to continue learning by increasing the capacity of your initial shot glass to something much bigger. This will, in turn, enhance your personal wiring diagram to a higher level of thinking than the level that got you in trouble in the first place.
- The greatest attributes for making progress are *humility* and *honesty*. Choose to continuously humble yourself and to not sugarcoat the truth and reality of your personal starting point. Life has a way of exposing those who fib about it while thinking they've got it all figured out.
- The greatest adversaries to making progress are *pride* and *procrastination*. Choosing to put the full-of-self pride on the sidelines today—not tomorrow—will serve you well. This will immediately kickstart and speed up the recovery process.
- The most precious commodity is *time*. It's available to all and extremely valuable, so don't waste it. Invest time in yourself by learning at every opportunity. Making deposits of precious nuggets of wisdom will pay you dividends your whole life.
- Put on your own oxygen mask first before trying to help others. This can be your personal health oxygen mask, your personal relationship oxygen mask, your personal freedom oxygen mask, your personal happiness oxygen mask, or your personal financial oxygen mask. Learn what it takes to improve yourself, reduce debt, and be self-sufficient first. You will then be better prepared to help others.

- Continue to gain understanding and make improvements in all areas of your life. Take ownership of where you are and how you got there. Take advantage of the B.O.W. improvement process to make things better. Pay it forward and share your story with others.

Thus began my personal path to improvement in all areas of my life. The result was the B.O.W. improvement process. Looking back, I realize that it was that initial belief of a better tomorrow that got things started for me, even if I didn't see right away the path to get out of the mess I was in. It was the belief that somehow, things would be OK. I didn't realize it at the time, but this belief, this vision of a better place, gave me the hope for a better tomorrow and the energy I needed to keep looking for the next steps forward.

I jotted these ideas down, as I wanted to share the outcome with others. I thought that if I could do it, then anyone should be able to do it. I just needed to identify the process that was silently working in the background, and somehow articulate it in a straightforward and simple way. I wanted to convey the idea of responsibility, accountability, and honesty, as well as generating solutions to all kinds of situations we find ourselves in, from a place of understanding.

There will not be a bell ringing someplace nearby indicating there might be danger ahead. Neither will there be a sign that drops out of the sky pointing us in some direction to begin this process of getting ourselves out of the predicament we have found ourselves in. It is about challenging the status quo when approaching the adversity most people face, then taking specific steps to move forward in a positive direction. It is about making gradual gains toward our overall well-being. It is about understanding and following a process for improvement. It is about a better tomorrow.

It shouldn't be that hard, I thought to myself, or, *Just put one foot in front of the other*, as the expression goes. Although the words we speak absolutely matter, the fact remains that *talk is cheap*. What we *do* has a monumentally higher significance when it comes to making a noticeable impact on our lives for good or bad. So I decided to *do* this. I decided to write about what I did to overcome the obstacles I faced from one of the lowest points in my life. I decided to write down the recovery process and what I believe it takes to *begin from where you are*.

I narrowed down this three-step process using the acronym B.O.W.

Step #1: B = Believe

Wanting and *believing* are very different. Wanting is more like wishing or dreaming. Believing has a way of awakening hope and bringing it to life. It suggests that you have a chance of getting there. Now let's look back at the questions asked at the beginning of the book, but this time replace the word *want* with the word *believe* in those same questions. Have a look at the questions below with this minor change and think about the impact on your outlook.

- Do you *believe* you can be healthier?
- Do you *believe* you can have more joy in your life?
- Do you *believe* you can live with less stress?
- Do you *believe* you can have more meaningful relationships?
- Do you *believe* you can earn more money?
- Do you *believe* you can be a business owner?
- Do you *believe* you can be financially independent?
- Do you *believe* you can be debt-free?
- Do you *believe* you can have more free time?
- Do you *believe* you can own your dream house?
- Do you *believe* you can live in a better neighborhood?
- Do you *believe* you can go on more vacations?
- Do you *believe* you can retire more comfortably?
- Do you *believe* you can have more peace of mind?

- Do you *believe* you can be more charitable?
- Do you *believe* you can add more value to other people's lives?
- Do you *believe* you can be a better son, daughter, spouse, sibling, parent, friend, employee, employer, coworker, or teammate?
- Do you *believe* you can end up in heaven after you take your last breath on earth?

Essentially, do you believe things can get better for yourself? You may find that if you ask someone in your circle of influence these questions using the word *want*, there will be a general "yes" as the answer to all the questions. Now go ahead and ask the same person the same questions using the word *believe* instead of *want*. You might not be surprised to find that not everyone believes it could happen, although most everyone wanted it to be so. Why would that be? Why would someone not believe it could really happen for them, even though they wanted it to be so?

As an example, I asked someone if they *wanted* to one day live in a better neighborhood, and the answer was a resounding "Yes, of course." Then I asked if they *believed* it would happen for them some day in the future. Sadly, their answer was "I doubt it." Once I asked why they didn't believe it, the excuses started pouring out.

I suppose they really thought that they were telling me their reasons, but they just sounded like excuses to me. They were not even open to the possibility, so they didn't believe it. They were stuck with a limited, shot-glass mindset. Their wiring diagram had not been enhanced for a very long time. I concluded that they were not willing to take the time to learn how to remove the things standing in their way, so that they could eventually end up in a better neighborhood. It could have all started by believing that it was possible.

There are all kinds of variations in perceptions, according to each person's definition of a better neighborhood or what constitutes a dream house or what qualifies as a stress-free life. The main point here is whether someone believes it just might happen, or does not believe it could happen at all. As it turns out, believing or not believing is the main difference between people right off the bat, before anything else is pursued or examined further.

As simple as it sounds, believing in a better tomorrow, believing that a situation can be resolved, believing things will somehow be OK, and believing that your predicament can improve matters a lot. Believing is the beginning of your journey toward recovery. Believing is not merely wanting. Believing is not mere wishful thinking. Believing is not merely dreaming. Believing, even without seeing, is a choice. Believing is the first step in the B.O.W. improvement process. I encourage you to begin from where you are by choosing to believe. It worked for me, and it can work for you too.

Step #2: O = Observe

At first glance, the name of this step, Observe, may imply to some people that it's a passive step of taking a glance from a distance, but that is certainly not the case. This is the step where the actual work is done. This step is a call to action. This is where you become a learning machine that absorbs knowledge like a dry sponge soaks up water. This is where you're expected to do the things that will increase your knowledge for a brighter future. This is where value is added. This is where precious time is invested. This is where you observe, research, investigate, discuss, ask, ponder, consider, debate, evaluate, focus, deep dive, and expend energy looking into the matter at hand.

It's game time, and your number is called to perform. This is where your wiring diagram gets enhanced and the onboard computer situated between your ears gets reprogrammed. This is where you get to make deposits into yourself. This is where your limited-capacity shot glass is replaced by a full-size mug, then a five-gallon pail, then a barrel. I think you get the idea. Sitting down at a table to learn is like having a seat at a table where wisdom is served.

This is where the understanding of *how it's possible* takes root and grows. This is where you begin to know what to do next because you will be prepared. This is where the excuses have no merit in your vocabulary. This is where you begin to see positive results, and you will like it, so you will keep doing it. This is where the questions turn into answers and doubt begins to evaporate.

This is where the word *believe* from the same questions above will be replaced by the words *know how* in the answers to those questions. This is where you will have the confidence to move forward because you will know how to do it. This is where you will generate the answers from a place of understanding. Go ahead and read the following out loud while giving yourself permission for it to sink in.

- I *know how* I can be healthier.
- I *know how* I can have more joy in my life.
- I *know how* I can live with less stress.
- I *know how* I can have more meaningful relationships.
- I *know how* I can earn more money.
- I *know how* I can be a business owner.
- I *know how* I can be financially independent.
- I *know how* I can be debt-free.
- I *know how* I can have more free time.
- I *know how* I can own my dream house.
- I *know how* I can live in a better neighborhood.
- I *know how* I can go on more vacations.
- I *know how* I can retire more comfortably.
- I *know how* I can have more peace of mind.
- I *know how* I can be more charitable.
- I *know how* I can add more value to other people's lives.
- I *know how* I can be a better son, daughter, spouse, sibling, parent, friend, employee, employer, coworker, or teammate.
- I *know how* I can end up in heaven after I take my last breath on earth.

Believing that things can get better is only the first step. It's not enough by itself to get you the positive results you're looking for. After the first step, you have to follow up and proceed to the second step. Nobody gets a pass when it comes to the second step, as it doesn't just happen on its own. You have to put in the time and do the work for yourself. I encourage you to stay the course during the entire second step of the process. If you do, you will obtain something that nobody can ever take away from you, namely *knowledge,* and you will be better prepared to handle just about anything. When you know that you know, you can just smile because you're confident that you know.

Step #3: W = Will

Will you? Are you willing? These are simple questions that only you can answer. Nobody can make you do anything you're not willing to do. Will you commit the time and energy to find out what you don't know? Will you get off the sidelines and decide to act? Will you at least consider the possibilities? Will you make the decision to begin from where you are?

This third step is about determining the truth about your mental toughness. This is where your resolve is tested. This is where the mask comes off and the truth will be revealed by whether you will do anything, or you won't. This is where your personal definition of the word *determination* is exposed. When you look in the mirror, this is when you will know the truth about the substance below the surface of your facade. This is where you see for yourself whether your pride and ego get put aside to allow you to humble yourself and face the reality of your situation. What will you do?

This is where you realize that the desires of your heart are being challenged by the bad habits you've been hiding behind and that have plagued you for years. This is where you get to dig in your heels and decide that enough is enough. This is where your actions or inactions will speak volumes without you having uttered a single word. This is where you know in your heart that you will not accept barely getting by as a possible outcome for the rest of your life. This is where you know that you will not be denied progress, regardless of your present circumstances.

Will you keep wasting valuable time playing mindless video games, or will you make the most of your spare time to learn something that can help you? What about the countless hours spent on social media? Was that valuable time invested in yourself to help you get out of trouble? Will you keep coming up with excuses, or will you immediately act, cutting out needless expenses to get your spending habits under control? Will you decide to stick with an improvement plan, no matter what, or will you give up after a week because it's *too hard*? Will you have the courage to continue to help yourself so you can help others, or will you just take the easy way out?

Once you decide to proceed forward with your whole mind, body, and spirit, then go ahead and get used to making the following declarations. Note that the previous answers containing the words *know how* are replaced by the word *will*. This is where the healing begins because you're about to take action.

- I *will* be healthier.
- I *will* have more joy in my life.
- I *will* live with less stress.
- I *will* have more meaningful relationships.
- I *will* earn more money.
- I *will* be a business owner.
- I *will* be financially independent.
- I *will* be debt-free.
- I *will* have more free time.
- I *will* own my dream house.
- I *will* live in a better neighborhood.
- I *will* go on more vacations.

- I *will* retire more comfortably.
- I *will* have more peace of mind.
- I *will* be more charitable.
- I *will* add more value to other people's lives.
- I *will* be a better son, daughter, spouse, sibling, parent, friend, employee, employer, coworker, or teammate.
- I *will* end up in heaven after I take my last breath on earth.

Believing that things can get better is not enough. Observing and learning and having the confidence of knowing how things can get better is still not enough. You have to be willing to proceed and *implement the how*, in order to generate the positive results you're looking for. You have to take the third step and be *willing* to do what it takes. All three steps, in sequence, have to work together as a tug-of-war team pulling in the same direction at the same time.

These three simple yet powerful ideas are the ingredients that I have personally found to help me the most when I was seeking lasting improvements in any area of my life. I encourage you to consider these for yourself, as they may help you too. Yes, it will take some time, but things will get easier. One by one, the noticeable improvements will manifest themselves in your life, and you will like it.

Perhaps mistakes were made. Perhaps someone misled or cheated you. Perhaps something out of your control happened. Regardless of your personal predicament, you can choose to give yourself the gift of forgiveness and decide to move forward toward a better place. The thoughts you have about the situation matter. The words you speak about it also matter. The steps you take—what you do—from that point forward matter the most.

You may have heard the story about four people named Everybody, Somebody, Anybody, and Nobody. There was an important job to be done, and Everybody was sure that Somebody would do it. Anybody could have done it, but Nobody did it. It turns out that Everybody blamed Somebody when Nobody did what Anybody could have done.

It's what we *do* about the situations we find ourselves in that counts. We can't point the finger at anyone else. Stuff happens all the time, and we're not immune to it. It's how we react to every small or big thing that matters in the long run. It's how well prepared we are to handle the curveballs thrown our way that determines the quality and length of time for our recovery.

I want you to realize that things can improve dramatically, no matter where you happen to be in your life. I want you to experience the comfort, joy, and inner peace of knowing way down deep inside that you can be on the path to recovery, irrespective of your starting point. I want you to have the confidence that you absolutely have what it takes to act, so you end up in a better place. I want you to know for sure that you can help yourself, as well as make a positive impact in other people's lives.

The ball is in your court. It's up to you where you go from here. I challenge you to say out loud that *it's possible* to make things better for yourself and, by extension, others around you. It may be difficult, but it's not impossible. It may take some time, but remember that life is a marathon, not a sprint. Dare to have a look in the mirror, take a deep breath, pace yourself, and improve your situation. Start by believing, then learning, then be willing to go for it, making adjustments along the way, for as long as it takes.

Reflection Questions for Chapter 9:

1. What personal predicament do you believe can be improved?

   _____
   _____
   _____
   _____
   _____
   _____
   _____
   _____
   _____
   _____
   _____
   _____
   _____

2. Will you commit and begin from where you are?

   _____
   _____
   _____
   _____
   _____
   _____
   _____
   _____
   _____
   _____
   _____
   _____
   _____
   _____
   _____

10

THE MOST IMPORTANT THING—IT'S NOT ABOUT YOU

This chapter is the most important of all. It's where the rubber meets the road. It's where the buck stops. It's the point where push comes to shove. It's where positive effectiveness takes on a life of its own. It's where all this gets real. It's where self-worth and joy and peace and love simultaneously gain strength and meaning. It's where the truth is tested, and it will be worth your while to examine it for yourself until you know for sure. It's where your true character is revealed. It's where humility and wisdom begin. It's the place where gaining understanding of all things takes root.

Above all things, *seek first the kingdom of God and His righteousness, and all these things will be given to you as well.* This was the advice Jesus, God's only Son, gave to his followers as written in Matthew 6:33 of the Holy Bible.

Specifically, what were *all these things* that would be provided to them, you may ask? It's all those things that they were worried about, like food, clothing, shelter, protection, and all that other stuff going on in their lives at the time. Not surprisingly, *those things* happen to be all the same things that cause us to worry also. It's the standard of living for our day-to-day existence here on earth. They are all pretty much the same things we're trying to improve and secure in our own lives today.

As it turns out, humanity has not changed all that much during the past two millennia or so since Jesus spoke those words. Basic human needs were about the same then as they are now. Sure, lots of technological advancements have taken place since biblical times. However, given the current dire condition that's painfully obvious all over the globe today, I would make the argument that Jesus' advice given in Matthew 6:33 is more relevant today than it was back then. Things are certainly more convenient today, but many people seem to be lost in a vast sea of complexity and confusion, going nowhere fast.

We seem to live in a world where there is virtually no desire for anyone to merely consider, much less appreciate, the gargantuan importance of acknowledging God in our daily lives. There is little to virtually no understanding of who God really is. Many even question His existence. Generally speaking, there is minimal understanding of what it takes to get to heaven, and practically no apparent concern of hell.

In my humble opinion, this general lack of a relationship with God, the Creator of the universe, is the main source of the hopelessness manifesting itself around the globe today. The relentless pursuit of people going out of their way to diminish and even erase the truth of God's existence has resulted in this massively growing state of despair. People in general just don't want to be accountable. They simply discount, and don't even want to hear, what God has to say about anything.

The media is certainly avoiding this subject, and most people are simply buying whatever the media is selling. They keep talking about the state of growing problems all over the globe, yet not a single major network is coming close to suggesting that it may be due to people's rejection of God's existence. They don't want to even mention the possibility, because it's just not politically correct. It's unfortunate that so many people remain in this state of ignorance on this most important subject. Just close your eyes for a minute and try if you can to imagine the grand design of maintaining the earth, the sun, and the moon, all in midair and in perfect balance with one another, and in plain sight. Only a supernatural God who is way, way, way, above our understanding could have done that.

I've heard it said that social engineering can be referred to as the art of manipulating, influencing, and deceiving people. It's all about gathering all kinds of data about us so that they can appeal to our human nature of likes and dislikes to sell more of their stuff to us. There are big bucks involved, and we're guided around like a bunch of sheep toward their product without even realizing it. They would rather we just go with the flow and not ask too many questions. They would rather we not exercise any independent thinking at all.

After all the results of the studies come out, most will tell you what you want to hear, not what you need to hear. They will appeal to your subliminal consciousness with innuendos of instant gratification. Most will tell you that you can afford tens of thousands, even hundreds of thousands, of dollars in mortgage debt, credit card debt, student debt, and car debt, ignoring the fact that you can't even handle a $400 emergency. They seem to continue to lower the lending requirements so that more people with lower credit scores qualify for even more debt. Sounds like a pretty good plan for the wolves, but not so much for the sheep now trapped in this bondage of debt and despair.

The fact is that most people don't even want to hear the truth, much less face it. As the expression goes, truth hurts, so avoiding the truth seems to be a less painful option. Most don't want to know who God is, and it's the main reason His Son, Jesus, advised His followers to seek God first above all things. We all need God in our lives more than we realize—and a whole lot more than we care to admit. This is another one of those times where emphasis needs to be added:

> **We all need God in our lives more than we realize—
> and a whole lot more than we care to admit.**

Some consider the lunar landing from about fifty years ago as one of the greatest accomplishments in human history to date. Although there have been countless additional breakthroughs resulting from space exploration, we've learned that outer space is simply too big and too harsh for human beings to venture too far away from Earth. We are essentially no closer to having discovered any other planet or moon within our solar system, much less outside it, with those elements which are necessary to sustain life. To say that our planet Earth is unique would be a gross understatement.

The Hubble Telescope was launched into orbit in 1990 and continues to provide information to this day. It zooms in a circular orbit way above our atmosphere at an altitude of about 350 miles above the earth's surface. It is powered by the sun and circles the earth about fifteen times each day. Talk about going around in circles; at about 17,000 miles per hour, that's a lot of air miles.

With the Hubble's technology, we've been able to see distances of ten to fifteen billion light years deep into outer space, and we've been able to learn about other planets, galaxies, and seasonal patterns, as well as many other cool facts about the vastness of the observable universe. By the way, *only one* light year is the distance travelled while moving at the speed of light for a whole year. Keep in mind that the light from the sun reaches the earth in only about eight minutes and nineteen seconds.

Can you possibly imagine moving at the speed of light for one whole year? How about trying to wrap your brain around moving at that same speed, not for 100 years, not for 1,000 years, not for one million years, but for ten or fifteen BILLION years, continuously and without any pit stops. That is really, really far out there. It's worth noting that among countless observations made to date from as far as the Hubble can see, there is nothing else out there like our special little planet Earth. What word would be suitable to describe this? Remarkable? Unique? Amazing? Breathtaking? Stunning? Unbelievable? Well, it's true. Earth is the only place able to sustain life. We're it.

It seems we're not quite satisfied yet. It seems we want to check out the action a few more billion light years farther out there. In light of Hubble's inability to discover other traces of life, its successor, the more advanced James Webb Space Telescope, is now scheduled to launch into orbit in 2021. We've decided we want to keep looking farther into space just to make sure. In addition, there is another proposal on the table of a giant high-definition space telescope (HDST), a kind of super–Hubble Space Telescope. If this proposal advances past the concept phase, then this multibillion-dollar flying object, with much larger mirrors twenty-four times sharper than those from Hubble, would be launched into orbit sometime in the 2030s.

The ultimate goal has always been to see if there are signs of alien life out there and perhaps answer the age-old question of whether we are alone in the cosmos. Ask yourself, *When will enough be enough*? Honestly ponder on whether looking out an additional 50 or 100 billion more light years in distance will help you make up your mind. What additional evidence can possibly be discovered that will cause you to be convinced of the absolute unique nature of our planet Earth? Despite all the data and intelligence gathered to date, *it is still claimed* that the birth of the universe came into existence via the Big Bang, some fourteen billion years ago, by mere chance. This is by far the biggest and most devastating deception in human history.

The Big Bang theory is, of course, the politically correct theory being taught to the masses as to how it all began. If this theory is carefully considered, how could anyone explain with any rationality the probability of Earth as we know it popping up to exist? I mean, does this not make you take notice and ask *why*? Among the countless galaxies and billions among billions of stars and planets observed out there, we're the only inhabitants right here on our special planet. The evidence continues to point to this fact, so whether people accept it or not is irrelevant.

What about all the other species living in harmony on this life-sustaining, self-preserving, perfectly balanced floating rock called Earth? Where is everybody else out there in space? Why did life only form here on earth? Does this even make you ask *what are the chances of that happening*? How much research have you personally conducted on this subject? How much blind faith would it take to believe in this evolution nonsense anyway? For anyone to consider the evolution account, it takes pure imagination, not faith.

No scientist on the planet, with all the benefits of technological advances in DNA research, can create a single living molecule from a bunch of nonliving chemical compounds, even trying to do so in the most controlled laboratory environments. Yet we're expected to believe that all of us complex living creatures, male and female, just evolved somehow by mere chance somewhere out there over eons of time. We all want to know where we came from, but if there was ever a time for common sense and independent thinking, this would be it.

Since the very early recordings about the heavens, people have looked to the stars, as many continue to do today, to refute the biblical account for supernatural, intelligent creation by God Himself. It's a frightening thought to most, because if the beginning of the universe as stated in Genesis 1:1 is true, it can be easily argued that the rest of the Bible is also true. If God really does exist, then perhaps we would do well to seek Him out first, and learn more about Him. This is why Jesus was advising his followers to humble themselves and find out more about the one and only supernatural God, Creator of all things.

The biblical account for all of creation only took seven days, and this set the weekly pattern with the last day being a day of rest. The day's pattern was designated by the earth's rotation around its axis. The month's pattern was designated by the moon's orbit around the earth, and the year's pattern was designated by the earth's orbit around the sun. It was all predesigned this way by God Himself, and that's how it all came to be. He was able to accomplish all this effortlessly. He alone is holy, which means He is in a distinct and separate category from us humans. We are, however, the pinnacle of His creation.

Given the fact that we can all walk around on our planet Earth, we can observe and study all that exists around us. We can witness the precision of each sunrise, and we can marvel at all the invisible forces that keep the earth in suspension, by perfect unexplainable design. These forces that exist didn't evolve because they're constant. They don't change. Science didn't invent or develop these constant forces. Science utilizes them because they're reliable and repeatable. They were purposefully meant to be exactly the way they are. They were all designed, created, and set in place by God Himself. It's the only logical explanation.

Knowing what we know to be true today, then how much faith would it take to believe that God Himself spoke the universe into existence along with all the requirements to keep it just so? This is the biblical account for the origin of everything that exists. Yes, it takes faith to believe in God as Creator, but it's not the amount of faith that matters; rather, it's the mere presence of it.

We were made in God's image, knowing good from bad, and we ought to have the common sense to realize that God must be way beyond our human understanding. He is a supernatural, eternal spirit, and He is the one who created us. We may know very few things about God, but we need to realize that He is infinite in every possible way. We will never know all there is to know about God. His thoughts and His works and His power and His understanding are all beyond any scale we can imagine. How proud and arrogant and foolish must some people be to think that they are owed some sort of explanation in order to fit God into their little shot-glass mindset? Yes, we have some understanding of God's attributes as being holy, sovereign, all-powerful, omniscient, and omnipresent, but that only scratches the surface. All we need to do is look around and see His awesome handiwork everywhere.

In our flawed humanity, we are intelligent enough, yet also generally so full of ourselves that we don't want to be accountable to a holy God who is also perfectly just. As a result, we continue to get bigger and more powerful space telescopes to look for someone else out there in an effort to disprove God's existence and thus eliminate His biblical account for supernatural creation. Most people simply want relief from the pain they're in without even considering looking toward the OEM—the Original Equipment Manufacturer—to get the answers. God designed each and every one of us, and He certainly knows us better than we know ourselves. The truth is that most people want to continue doing whatever they want, without any concern about something that was written long ago in an old book.

The fact remains that none of these space exploration efforts, along with their massive endless budgets, have delivered anything that many were hoping for. Many want to simply separate themselves from the reality of what they have observed and learned so far. When you look around, there seems to be a growing sense of desperation around the world, perhaps because the truth is being revealed and people in general are rejecting it. If the billions of people on our planet Earth don't acknowledge God's existence, then is it any wonder that there is so much pain and discord in the world today?

If you believe, as I do, that everything happens for a reason, then you have to believe that you were meant to read this little book at this very moment. Merely acknowledging God's existence is not equivalent to having some sort of gate pass into heaven. Being a good person won't do it either. Keep learning with an honest and humble heart until you know for sure. Continue to grow in your knowledge and investigate for yourself the true meaning of the acronym T.U.L.I.P.

T = Total Depravity
U = Unconditional Election
L = Limited Atonement
I = Irresistible Grace
P = Preservation of the Saints

Why the strong emphasis in this last chapter? Why is this the most important thing? The simple answer is because humanity is called to return to and reestablish a relationship with the Creator Himself. For our own good, we ought to have at least a basic understanding of where we came from. Like all the other items we've covered so far, making decisions from a place of understanding will help guide us in the right direction. It puts everything into proper perspective.

It all starts with where you stand on the subject of creation or evolution, so that's the reason this is the most important thing to get right before anything else we may pursue in this life. Every single person who is mature enough to think independently is faced with this option. You either believe God created the heavens and the earth, or you don't. I would not be doing you any favors if I didn't mention that you owe it to yourself to invest the time it takes to look into it until you know for sure. You already know where I stand.

I've noticed that, in general, people who acknowledge God's existence and presence have more joy in their lives. They may not always be happy about this or that, but they very rarely lose their joy. They experience life's ups and downs just like everyone, but they seem to keep a *big picture* perspective in mind. The more a person learns about the true nature of God, the more joy they experience in life.

It's worth noting the distinction between *happiness* and *joy*, as they are not the same.

- Happiness depends on your circumstances, situations, conditions, and surroundings, all of which can change

without notice. Difficulty, hardship, and pain are only temporary. One's mood swings from high to low—happy to unhappy—are based on changing circumstances in things like health, an accident, more stuff, less stuff, etc. Happiness comes and goes.
- Joy depends on relationships. For those who know God, circumstances may change, but the relationship with Jesus and the Spirit in the believer's heart will help him or her maintain their joy. Joy comes from the personal relationship with Jesus, knowing that nothing can shake you out of His hands, all because of who God is. Joy is a spiritual gift. The fruit of the Holy Spirit, as written in Galatians 5:22–23, is love, joy, peace, patience, kindness, goodness, faithfulness, gentleness, and self-control. You can have joy even in times of suffering because you know that God, the Creator of the universe, is in control of all things.

Sure, everyone wants to be happy. It's everyone's right to pursue happiness, and so you should. The question is, do you have joy in your heart, regardless of your situation? Joy is not just a feeling, but it's the confidence of knowing without a doubt that the Holy Spirit dwells in your heart by the grace of God. It's a truth that never changes regardless of the changing circumstances.

I started by sharing with you how I arrived at the B.O.W. process for improvement. Yes, *I believed* that God exists, but I didn't really understand many things about Him at first. Then, *I observed* for myself. In retrospect, I felt drawn to observe and investigate. I took the time to research, and I began to realize how little I actually knew about Him. Then, *I was willing* to learn more, and my understanding of *all the other things* increased in clarity, and became easier to deal with. I learned that if I approached God with a humble heart, He would always be faithful to reveal Himself to me. I believe that you can do the same.

I also mentioned that gaining understanding was the foundation to making improvements to all areas of life, and that time was the most precious commodity. It would be wise for us to take the time and ask God to reveal Himself to us. We ought to have a humble heart and ask Him to forgive our prideful nature when we don't acknowledge Him. God also wants us to be in heaven with Him and made it possible for us to do so.

The Bible teaches that the only way into heaven is believing that God's only Son, Jesus, left the majesty of heaven, came to earth and took our place, being the only One who could pay the price for our sins by taking on God's perfectly just wrath. The path to heaven is afforded to us by God's grace, through faith in Jesus the Son. Jesus suffered and died in our place, then He rose again conquering death, so that anyone who believes in Him, would end up in eternal heaven after life on earth ends. This is the best news for all of humanity. We ought to learn about the nature of God, His kingdom, and His righteousness *so that all these other things* will be provided to us as well.

So it began for me some years ago to the point where I am today. The journey isn't over because I'm still breathing. Making things better is a continuous, lifelong process. God has commanded us to be strong and courageous. He also commanded us not to be afraid or discouraged, because He will be with us wherever we go. If you have God in your life, there is no greater ally and friend you could ever possibly have.

God's armor for our daily lives consists of a belt representing truth, a breastplate representing righteousness, shoes representing peace, a shield representing faith, a helmet representing salvation from eternal damnation, and the sword of the Spirit representing God's Word, the Holy Bible. Irrespective of your past, it's never too late to ask God for forgiveness, to believe in His Son Jesus' death and resurrection, and to ask for His presence in your life.

I have learned that a person may certainly have a full life, as represented by the full glass jar from the Psychology 101 class. The jar may be full of health, family, friends, home, jobs, businesses, cars, furniture, vacations, investments, sports, hobbies, and all that other stuff that happens in life. It's worth noting that the glass jar is still extremely fragile, and it can shatter without notice. God ought to be the first to be placed in your jar of life. God is also the only solid foundation on which the jar ought to be placed. Everything will work better once you place your whole life in God's hands. After all, He created the entire universe and all of us living creatures. You would be wise to build this foundation first. Dare to approach His throne with unwavering faith, humility, and gratitude; then with confidence, you can begin from where you are.

MAY GOD, CREATOR OF ALL THAT EXISTS, BLESS YOU AND KEEP YOU, NOW AND ALWAYS!

Reflection Questions for Chapter 10:

1. Do you believe that God created the entire universe and that God's Son, Jesus, died and rose again in order to forgive you, so you can have access to heaven?

   _____
   _____
   _____
   _____
   _____
   _____
   _____
   _____
   _____
   _____
   _____

2. Based on your understanding of who God is and your relationship with Him, do you know for sure that you will end up in heaven after you take your last breath on Earth?

   _____
   _____
   _____
   _____
   _____
   _____
   _____
   _____
   _____
   _____
   _____
   _____
   _____